Did St Paul
Get Jesus
Right?

Did St Paul Get Jesus Right?

The Gospel According to Paul

LION

David Wenham

A Lion Book
an imprint of
Lion Hudson plc
Wilkinson House, Jordan Hill Road,
Oxford OX2 8DR, England
www.lionhudson.com
ISBN 978 0 7459 6248 1

Distributed by:
UK: Marston Book Services, PO Box 269, Abingdon, Oxon, OX14 4YN
USA: Trafalgar Square Publishing, 814 N. Franklin Street, Chicago, IL 60610
USA Christian Market: Kregel Publications, PO Box 2607, Grand Rapids,
MI 49501

First edition 2010
10 9 8 7 6 5 4 3 2 1 0
All rights reserved

Acknowledgments
pp. 27, 28, 47, 75, 85, 88, 93: Scripture quotations taken from the *Holy Bible, New
International Version,* copyright © 1973, 1978, 1984 International Bible Society.
Used by permission of Zondervan and Hodder & Stoughton Limited. All rights
reserved. The 'NIV' and 'New International Version' trademarks are registered in
the United States Patent and Trademark Office by International Bible Society. Use
of either trademark requires the permission of International Bible Society. UK
trademark number 1448790.
All other Scripture quotations are the author's own translation.

This book has been printed on paper and board independently certified
as having been produced from sustainable forests.

A catalogue record for this book is available
from the British Library

Typeset in 11/14 Garamond
Printed and bound in Great Britain by J F Print Ltd., Sparkford, Somerset

Contents

Preface 7

Chapter 1 What is the Question and Why is it Important? 9

Chapter 2 Can We Use the New Testament as Evidence? 16

Chapter 3 How Paul Got Jesus... or How Jesus Got Paul: The Evidence on Paul's Conversion 25

Chapter 4 Was Paul Interested in the Real Jesus? Evidence from Corinth on the Crucifixion and Resurrection 40

Chapter 5 Sex, Apostleship, and Love: More Evidence from Corinth and Beyond 55

Chapter 6 "Abba", and What Happens When We Die: Evidence from Galatia and Thessalonica 69

Chapter 7 Was Paul the Inventor of Christian Doctrines? 80

Chapter 8   Did Paul and Jesus Really Agree?   97

Chapter 9   Is Paul Behind the New Testament
             Gospels?   124

Chapter 10   But Paul Was Certainly a
             Controversialist   138

Chapter 11   So Did Paul Get Jesus Right?   148

             Notes   157

Preface

Sensational stories about the origins of Christianity appear in the media with unfailing regularity. In recent years we have heard that:

- Christianity was originally a psychedelic mushroom cult.

- Jesus married Mary Magdalene and had a child, or several children – a story successfully suppressed by the church.

- The Gospel of Judas has been found which seems to vindicate Judas, the disciple who betrayed Jesus.

Such stories sell books and make good films, but they almost always represent at best a fanciful reading of the evidence. Indeed there is often rather little evidence, and what there is is culpably misused.

Some of the books that have recently caught the headlines deliberately mix history and fantasy. Dan Brown's *The Da Vinci Code* has the hero and heroine racing from scene to scene cracking codes and discovering dark conspiracies in the Catholic church. They find, among other things, that Jesus was married, that the idea of Jesus as Son of God was not established until the fourth century AD, and that there were other gospels than those of the church, which gave a very different account of Jesus from that officially approved by the church.

More recently, in Philip Pullman's *The Good Man Jesus and the Scoundrel Christ* Mary has twins, one called Jesus and the other – a much less attractive child – called Christ. In discussing the background to his novel, Pullman contrasts the real historical Jesus (the good man) with the Christ of St Paul and the church (represented in his fictional story by the "scoundrel Christ"). Paul doctored and skewed the original story of Jesus, turning the man Jesus into the divine Christ; and it is this version of Christianity that the church adopted and has followed ever since.

Although both Brown and Pullman are explicitly writing fiction, they both bring in ideas about the origins of Christianity which they, as authors, take seriously. And readers have understandably been confused as to what is fact and what is fiction.

In the face of such confusion this book tries to help. It touches on many of the questions mentioned, but looks particularly at the widespread view that Paul skewed the story of Jesus and, in effect, founded a different religion from that of Jesus. It is intended for readers, Christian and other, who want to look carefully at the question of Paul and Jesus, and who want to distinguish the fact from the fiction. The book is not an entertaining page-turner like *The Da Vinci Code*. But I have tried to make it readable and to avoid being over-technical. I hope that readers will have the patience to follow the argument through, to consider the evidence, and to weigh the conclusions, which I believe to be very important.

I have deliberately not loaded this book with references, but I have noted some important ones in endnotes, so that readers who wish to can check the evidence being cited.

I am very grateful to all the friends who have commented on this book and have helped to make it better than it was.

CHAPTER 1

What is the Question and Why is it Important?

The history of the world is a story of power struggles – between tribes, nations, empires, and ideologies. Today is no different from the past: there are military conflicts, political and economic rivalries, and ideological wars between the religions and other belief systems. These include Marxism and communism (at present on the wane), other forms of atheism and materialism (not at all on the wane), religious fundamentalism (of various sorts), postmodernism, and paganism. The great religions of the world are still competing strongly: Islam is obviously in the ascendant. Hinduism arguably has a modern reincarnation in postmodernism, and Christianity, though declining in the West, is growing in other parts of the world.

Military and political struggles feature all the time on our television screens, and it is easy to see how important and dangerous they are, not just to those living in war zones, but to the whole world. The ideological wars are not always so visible or so easily portrayed in the media, though they are often bound up with politics (as in the Middle East). But they are also very important. Richard Dawkins and the "new atheists" may be wrong about many things, but in this respect they are right: they recognize that the struggles going on in our modern world for the hearts and minds of human beings matter; the outcomes will be of huge importance for the future of human society and indeed of our planet.

In today's ideological battles certain issues regularly come to the fore, and this book is looking at one of the key points where Christianity has often been under attack in recent years. It concerns St Paul (as Christians call him) and his relationship to Jesus.

Who were Jesus and Paul?

Jesus was a Jew who lived in Palestine in the first part of the first century AD. A healer, a teacher, and the founder of a popular movement, he became by any reckoning a hugely important figure. His followers, who were initially all Jews, came to see him as their "messiah" whom their Scriptures, the so-called Old Testament, told them about. The word "messiah" means "anointed one", and the Old Testament spoke of God sending an anointed king who would save the Jewish people from their enemies and bring peace and prosperity. Jesus' followers saw him as that saviour.

Jesus was opposed by people in power, both the Jewish authorities and the Romans, who ruled Palestine, and he was finally crucified. But his movement did not die with him. His followers claimed that he rose from the dead two days after his crucifixion and that his death was a sacrifice, bringing the forgiveness of people's sins. They started to proclaim him as "Lord" and "Son of God" around the

Mediterranean world. Christians have gone on making these claims ever since.

If this is the Christian story of Jesus, who was Paul? He was one of the most important figures in the Jesus movement in its earliest days. He helped shape the church as it evolved; he was at the forefront of its missionary outreach; and a large part of the Christian New Testament was written by him or about him. He should probably be considered as second only to Jesus (with apologies to Peter) among people who influenced the development of Christianity.

The accusation against Paul and his inventive imagination

But this is precisely the issue that this book is intending to address, because Paul is frequently accused of not being a faithful interpreter of Jesus, but distorting Jesus' message almost out of all recognition. It is alleged that Paul and others turned Jesus, who was no more than a popular Jewish teacher and healer from Palestine, into a divine cult figure who came down from heaven to save humankind, died as a blood sacrifice for the sins of the world, was raised from the dead and ascended into heaven, and who will one day return to judge the world.

Paul turns out to be the author of key Christian doctrines, so the argument goes, and the founder of Christianity as we know it. But the religion that he created was not that of Jesus. It was something constructed out of the story of Jesus through Paul's own imagination: he was influenced by the pagan religions of the Greek world (for example the mystery religions with their ideas of gods dying and rising) and most of all by his own experience of conversion to Christianity on the road to Damascus, when he claimed to have seen, heard, and been called by Jesus. His imagined view of Jesus dominated the early church, and the real Jesus, it is claimed, lost out.

Does it matter?

If this view of Paul is true, then the case for Christianity in the market-place of ideas is greatly weakened. It is unlikely that many people would want to go on believing in a Jesus produced by Paul's imagination. It is also unlikely that a relatively ordinary Palestinian prophet and teacher from the first century, if this is what Jesus really was, would command much of a following today.

So the view in question is a very serious attack on Christianity. It is also a subtle attack, since at first sight it does not look like an attack on what is most sacred to Christians – Jesus himself. It looks like an attack on something – or someone – of much less importance.

And this attack on Paul is appealing to all sorts of people, including those who find him problematic for other reasons:

- Jews have seen Paul as a traitor because of his conversion.

- Muslims revere Jesus, but do not like Paul's insistence that Jesus was the Son of God.

- Modern people often see Paul as misogynistic and homophobic.

- Modern people are also sceptical of the Christian church as an institution, and find conspiracy theories about it and its origins very attractive.

Some Christians find Paul difficult for these and other reasons, and separating Paul from Jesus may feel like a relief rather than a threat to their faith. It can be seen as positively advantageous in the modern multi-faith world not to have to defend the divinity and uniqueness of Jesus.

Is the attack on Paul justified?

But, if this attack on Paul is serious and appealing, is it justified? There have been many popular proponents of the idea, such as the novelist Philip Pullman. But there have also been scholars who have supported it. Over a hundred years ago the German William Wrede put forward something like this view in his book *Paul*.[1] In more recent years the Jewish scholar Hyam Maccoby wrote a book with the self-explanatory title *The Mythmaker: Paul and the Invention of Christianity*.[2]

It would be easy to suppose that if any scholars, and especially Christian scholars, held such a view they must have had a good reason for doing so. But it would be unwise to conclude that too quickly. There are scholars who deny the Holocaust, or deny climate change, or believe that the earth is just a few thousand years old. Intelligent people used to believe that the earth was flat. Scholars can be found who deny almost anything, including most aspects of traditional Christian belief. But the question is: are they right? What are the arguments?

This short book is an attempt, by someone who has been interested in the question for a long time, to show that Paul did not invent Christianity or change the religion of Jesus, but that he got Jesus right.[3]

Where are we going? An outline of the contents of this book

Although this book is a short one, the journey it takes is quite long, looking at the various questions and issues that scholars and others have raised.

• Chapter 2 looks at the important preliminary question of whether the New Testament is usable at all as historical evidence.

• Chapter 3 considers Paul's conversion and the possibility that this could be the source of his ideas about Jesus, for example his view of Jesus as divine.

• Chapters 4 to 6 address the question of why Paul seems to refer to Jesus' life and teaching so little. Was Paul not interested in the real Jesus, but only in his own mystical experience? These three chapters assemble some of the most important evidence for Paul's knowledge of Jesus.

• Chapter 7 looks specifically at where Paul got his views about Jesus' divinity and Jesus' death.

• Chapter 8 asks if Paul and Jesus were really in agreement, or whether their religions were quite different.

• Chapter 9 considers Paul's influence on the rest of the

New Testament, and how far the New Testament is his version of Christianity.

- Chapter 10 reviews the main arguments, and comes back to the big question: did Paul get Jesus right?

CHAPTER 2

Can We Use the New Testament as Evidence?

Much of the argument of this book will involve careful study of evidence from the Christian New Testament. But some readers may wonder: is this in any way acceptable as evidence? Or am I, as a Christian scholar, simply assuming that the Christian Bible is true?

It is often said by "new atheists" such as Richard Dawkins that science works with evidence but faith does not – almost by definition. That view is a very prejudiced one; faith may sometimes be blind, but is often firmly based on evidence. In this book I will not simply be assuming the truth of the Bible but arguing a serious historical case on the basis of serious historical evidence.

So, before embarking on a study of Paul, we need as a preliminary to say something about whether the New Testament can be seen as such historical evidence. Many people imagine that it has no credibility as history. But that view usually arises out of ignorance.

Five general points are worth making here.

1. Ancient history is not all bunk!

Quite a lot of ancient history is lost. We do not know what happened, and at best can only guess and speculate. Sometimes, however, there is plenty of very good evidence, and we know a lot.

This is true of the Roman empire around the time when the Christian movement began. There are some excellent written historical sources, and plenty of significant archaeological evidence. So we know that Julius Caesar, the Roman general and emperor, went to Britain: he wrote a historical account of his campaign in the *Gallic Wars*. As well as such written records of the Romans in Britain, there are notable archaeological remains dating from after Caesar's time, for example the baths at Bath and the great wall built by the emperor Hadrian across Cumbria and Northumberland. So we have serious historical evidence enabling us to speak confidently, even if not very extensively, about events and life in Roman Britain.

2. The New Testament in the Roman first century

Jesus and the church started out in Palestine, which was also a part of the Roman empire. The church grew and spread in all directions, but the New Testament only documents its growth within the Mediterranean region and within the empire.

The picture provided by the New Testament fits again and again with what is known from other historical sources.

Those sources include:

- the fine Roman historian Tacitus, who wrote about AD 100: he refers to Christians in Rome during the reign of the emperor Nero in AD 64 and calls Christianity a "mischievous superstition". He also refers to Jesus as the Christians' founder and to his crucifixion under Pontius Pilate, the Roman governor also referred to in the New Testament.

- another Roman historian, Suetonius, who refers to Jews being expelled from Rome by the emperor Claudius, probably in AD 49, an event again mentioned in the New Testament. It referes to two friends of Paul, Aquila and Priscilla, having come to Greece from Rome "because Claudius had ordered all the Jews to leave Rome".[1]

- the Jewish historian Josephus, who wrote two histories about the Jewish people. He described Palestine and events there in the time of Jesus and the early Christian church, having lived there himself until about AD 68. He refers to many of the people who feature in the New Testament, including Jesus himself, John the Baptist, Herod the Great, Pontius Pilate, the high priest Caiaphas, and so on. He also talks about groups such as the Pharisees and the Samaritans. Josephus tells us much that is not found in the New Testament, for example about the disastrous mistakes made by Pilate, but he is clearly writing about the same people and the same world as are described in the New Testament.

- archaeological finds, for example:
  - an inscription found on the coast of Palestine that refers to the Roman emperor Tiberius and to Pilate the governor;

- an ornate ossuary, probably containing the bones of Caiaphas found in 1990 (an ossuary is a box in which the bones of the dead were stored after their bodies had decomposed);

- an inscription at Delphi in Greece referring to Gallio, proconsul (or governor) of Achaia in the south of modern Greece during the reign of Claudius. This Gallio is also mentioned in the Acts of the Apostles, where it says that Paul was brought before him in the city of Corinth and charged with trouble-making. The inscription is especially useful since it can be dated to about AD 52 and so enables us to put a date on Paul's visit to Corinth, and then on other events in the New Testament.

Corroboration of the New Testament: some examples

Josephus, a Jewish historian born about AD 37, confirms what the gospels say about John the Baptist, the popular Jewish prophet who baptized Jesus at the beginning of his ministry:

"John, surnamed the Baptist... he was a good man and had exhorted the Jews to lead righteous lives... and so doing to join in baptism... Herod had put him to death."

Antiquities, 18.116–119

Tacitus, a Roman historian who lived about AD 56 to 120, refers to the crucifixion:

"Christus... suffered the extreme penalty during the reign of Tiberius at the hands of one of our procurators, Pontius Pilatus,

and a most mischievous superstition, thus checked for the
moment, again broke out."
Annals, XV.44.2–8

Gallio is mentioned in the New Testament book of Acts (18:12).
He also appears in a stone inscription in which the Roman
emperor Claudius refers to:

"Junius Gallio my friend, and proconsul..."

What is quite clear from this evidence is that the New
Testament writings are not theological fairy-tales or fiction.
Their descriptions of Jesus, the early Christians and their
context make very good sense, whether it is fishing boats on
the Lake of Galilee or the horrible business of crucifixion
in Jerusalem, or conflict between Jewish religious groups
or travel around the Mediterranean world. Those who say
that the New Testament books are all partisan Christian
accounts that are not corroborated by other sources are
wrong, though it is true that the Romans were not at first
very interested in the new religious movement that had
begun in a remote corner of their empire.

3. First-century documents and early first-century documents

The New Testament is a collection of twenty-seven
Christian writings, some of them "gospels" – accounts of
Jesus' life and ministry – and many of them letters. They
have all been minutely and critically examined by scholars,
both Christian and other, some of whom are very sceptical.

These scholars have all kinds of views about the documents. But what is agreed almost universally is that all the books in our New Testament go back to the first century AD, and that some of them were written within decades of Jesus' death. Jesus was probably crucified in AD 30, plus or minus a year or two. So our earliest written sources come from very soon after the time of Jesus. The popular misconception that the New Testament was written centuries after the time of Jesus is unfounded.

The Contents of the New Testament

Four gospels ("gospel", in Greek *euangelion*, means "good news")
- Matthew
- Mark
- Luke
- John

A history of the early church
- The Acts of the Apostles (written by the author of Luke's Gospel)

Letters from Paul to churches and individuals
To the churches in:
- Rome
- Corinth (southern Greece), two letters
- Galatia (mid Turkey)
- Ephesus (western Turkey)
- Philippi (northern Greece)
- Colosse (near Ephesus)
- Thessalonica (northern Greece), two letters

To individuals:
- Timothy, two letters
- Titus
- Philemon

Letters by people other than Paul
- Hebrews (author unknown)
- James
- Peter, two letters

A vision
- Revelation

---

4. Doctored texts?

A common concern is that the writings of the New
Testament may have been distorted or tampered with over
the course of the centuries. Clearly this is a theoretical
possibility, since we do not have the originals and
since copies were made by hand, not mechanically or
electronically. However, the evidence suggests that ancient
scribes were remarkably accurate in their copying, and
classical scholars do not have many serious doubts about
the accuracy of the texts of historians such as Tacitus
and Caesar, even though the earliest copies we have of
their works date from a thousand years after the original
writing.

With the New Testament we have copies – large numbers
of copies – going back to the second and third centuries
AD, with one small section of John's Gospel being dated
by the experts to around AD 125. This fragment, now in
Manchester, is astonishingly early.

Although there are occasional uncertainties about wording, we can be confident that we have a reliable text of the New Testament, so that when we are reading Mark's Gospel or Paul's letters we are reading what the authors wrote (or dictated). There is no evidence indicating significant tampering with the texts.

Dates of Texts and Manuscripts

- Thucydides, Greek historian writing 400 BC: earliest manuscript tenth century AD
- Tacitus, Roman historian writing AD 100: first manuscript ninth century AD
- New Testament – 5,000 manuscripts, going back to the second, third, and fourth centuries AD

---

5. Intelligent authors

A final observation worth making is that the writers of the New Testament were intelligent! Sometimes modern writers assume – with an unfortunate arrogance – that ancient writers and ancient people generally were unsophisticated, uneducated, uncritical and gullible. Some, of course, were, but then so are some people today. But a lot of people in the Roman world were far from gullible; there were atheists and sceptics, as today; and many ancient authors were well-educated, sophisticated, and critical. Modern classical historians have a high regard for the Greek historian Thucydides and the Roman historian Tacitus, to mention two.

The author of Luke's Gospel writes at the start of having followed everything "accurately from the beginning", of

eyewitnesses, of wanting to write a "reliable account".[2]
He clearly wants to impress his readers with his historical
accuracy. This could all be for show, of course, though we
shall see evidence later for thinking it was more than that.
But in any case his words reveal an educated and self-aware
author who thought about what he was doing.

Conclusion

We have said enough to set out on our investigation of Paul.
We have not looked at all the historical issues relating to
the New Testament; that would require a different book, or
series of books! What has been shown so far is that some
of the popular doubts about the New Testament being
remote from the actual events or historically doubtful are
misplaced, and we can proceed to look at the evidence
relating specifically to the question of Paul and Jesus.

CHAPTER 3

How Paul Got Jesus… or How Jesus Got Paul: The Evidence on Paul's Conversion

Paul's conversion on the road to Damascus is surely the most famous religious conversion of all time. And there is no doubt that it was a hugely formative event in Paul's life and thinking. Was it this event that persuaded Paul of Jesus' divinity, and was Paul then the person who introduced this idea to the Christian church?

To answer these questions, it is necessary to review what happened at Paul's conversion.

Sources of information: how do we know about Paul's conversion?

The main sources of information about what happened on the Damascus road are the book of Acts and Paul's letter to the Galatians. Acts is a history of the earliest days of the Christian church; we do not know for certain who wrote it, but it is quite clear from its opening words (about "my first volume") and its dedication that it was written by the same person who wrote Luke's Gospel.[1] That person has been identified from at least the second century AD with Luke, a companion of Paul (referred to as "Luke the doctor" in Paul's letter to the Colossians).[2]

Some people are not sure about the identification. But what makes it seem thoroughly likely is the fact that the author of Acts drops into the first person – "we did" this and that – about half-way through his book, when he is describing Paul's travels. Up to that point the author has said "they did" this and that, but then he switches to "we". It has been suggested that he starts using someone else's diary, or that the shift is just to add a dramatic quality to the story. But easily the most obvious explanation is that the author was there and was indeed a companion of Paul.[3]

The fact that more than half of Acts is about Paul and his travels lends weight to this view, as does the author's detailed knowledge of the geography of the Mediterranean world. Scholars have shown that in describing Paul's travels the author of Acts gets the routes right – not so easy in a world without atlases or the internet. And he gets details to do with individual places right, such as the names of local officials.

So the case for Luke being the author of Acts is extremely strong. If it is correct, then this means that we have an account of Paul's conversion from a first-century writer. He had first-hand knowledge of Paul and, moreover, declares his intention to write a well-researched and reliable account of things.

Paul's letter to the Galatians is another very early account of Paul's conversion, probably written in the late AD 40s, though some people place it later, in the 50s. Either way it is an early account – Jesus was crucified about AD 30, and Paul's conversion was probably a couple of years later. Furthermore it is direct testimony, since there is no reasonable doubt that this fiery and emotional letter was written by Paul himself to churches that he founded in Galatia – part of modern Turkey.

The fact that Galatians was written by Paul, and indeed that Acts was written by a friend of Paul, does not necessarily mean that these accounts of Paul's conversion are trustworthy. Both writers could be putting a particular spin on what happened. But there is good reason to doubt that, since Paul hardly comes out of either account with great credit.

The accounts of Paul's conversion in the Bible

Luke's narrative in Acts

> Meanwhile, Saul was still breathing out murderous threats against the Lord's disciples. He went to the high priest and asked him for letters to the synagogues in Damascus, so that if he found any there who belonged to the Way, whether men or women, he might take them as prisoners to Jerusalem. As he neared Damascus on his journey, suddenly a light from heaven flashed around him. He fell to the ground and heard a voice say to him, "Saul, Saul, why do you persecute me?" "Who are you, Lord?" Saul asked. "I am Jesus, whom you are persecuting," he replied. "Now get up and go into the city, and you will be told what you must do."
>
> Acts 9:1–6

Paul's own comments on his conversion

For you have heard of my previous way of life in Judaism, how
intensely I persecuted the church of God and tried to destroy it. I
was advancing in Judaism beyond many Jews of my own age and
was extremely zealous for the traditions of my fathers. But when
God, who set me apart from birth and called me by his grace, was
pleased to reveal his Son in me so that I might preach him among
the Gentiles, I did not consult any man.

Galatians 1:13–16

So what seems to have happened?

Paul's background

Paul came from a devoutly Jewish family who lived in
Tarsus in south Turkey; the family were from the tribe of
Benjamin, which is probably why Paul's first name was Saul
(this was the name of the first Jewish king, who was also
from that tribe). Saul is a Hebrew name. But it was normal
for Jewish families living outside Palestine in areas where
Greek was used to give their children a Roman or Greek
name too; in this case it was Paulus (in Latin) or Paulos (in
Greek) – Paul. The family seem to have had some standing
in their local non-Jewish community, having been granted
Roman citizenship – a relatively unusual privilege for people
living outside Italy. So Paul grew up in two cultures and
speaking several languages fluently, probably including
Aramaic (the common language of the Jews), Hebrew (the
ancient language of the Jews), Greek, and some Latin.

His family sent the young Saul to Jerusalem to be given a

good Jewish education in a Pharisaic school. Acts says that he studied under the leading rabbi Gamaliel. The Pharisees were a relatively small but influential group of Jews who were rigorously committed to upholding the Jewish way of life and religion. The Jews were politically, militarily, and economically dominated by the mighty, wealthy and often glamorous Romans, and they were very sensitive to the religious and moral threat represented by their superpower overlords. The Pharisees were something like the orthodox Muslims in the Middle East today in their desire to maintain their religious traditions and religious purity. Some were more liberal, some more fundamentalist. Paul was a "zealous" Pharisee as a student, who was brilliant, very religious, and outdid his class-mates in his commitment to the cause.[4]

It was this that led to his becoming one of the arch-enemies of the Christian movement. This movement was very young. Its founder, Jesus, had come into conflict with the Pharisees because he was liberal (as the Pharisees saw it). He did not follow their strict interpretation of the law on issues such as keeping the Jewish Sabbath, and he mixed with the kind of ordinary sinful people from whom the Pharisees tried to keep separate. (The name "Pharisee" probably means "separatist".)

Jesus was now dead, crucified by the Romans. But his followers, far from giving up, were announcing that he had come to life again and that he was the messiah, whom all good Jews were awaiting. The movement was gaining a lot of support, in Jerusalem itself and beyond, to the distress of the Jewish authorities. Their attempts to suppress it, including by arresting and killing some of its leaders, were

The Mediterranean world
at the time of Paul

singularly unsuccessful. It was in this context that the student Paul began to get involved, and in due course he became one of the most violent and feared opponents of the Christians.

We know something of the viciousness of religious fundamentalists in our world, not least in the Middle East. They feel justified in taking drastic action against what they see as error and against those who are propounding it. So Paul says of himself: "I was violently persecuting the church of God and was trying to destroy it."[5] Luke's account is that he was "ravaging the church, going into house after house; dragging off both men and women, he committed them to prison."[6] Acts gives the impression that he was a major factor in causing Christians to flee from Jerusalem. And then he went in pursuit, getting authorization from the religious authorities in Jerusalem to go to Damascus, in Syria, where some of the Christians had gone, and to bring them forcibly to Jerusalem for whatever fate might await them.

His extraordinary conversion

It was in the context of this brutal mission that Paul had his famous "Damascus road" conversion. As Luke describes the event it seems as though:

- Paul experienced "a light from heaven", which left him temporarily blind.

- He collapsed on the ground.

- He heard – or thought he heard – a voice saying "Saul, Saul, why are you persecuting me?" He then identified the voice as that of Jesus, who told him to go on into Damascus.

- He did so, and his sight was restored by one of the Christians in Damascus, called Ananias. Paul began his new life as a Christian, getting baptized and beginning to preach on the Christian side.[7]

This is a plausible enough account of what Paul experienced, or at least thought that he experienced. Although Luke obviously admires Paul (and is his companion), the account of him before his conversion is harsh. Paul was a fearsome individual, and it is clear that the Christians (Ananias included) found it very difficult to believe that he was genuinely converted and welcome him as their Christian brother. Paul's own account of what happened also fits with what Luke tells us (not surprisingly, especially if Luke got the story from Paul). It is equally unflattering: he speaks more than once in his letters of his violent persecution of the Christians, and he is extremely conscious therefore of how extraordinary it was that Jesus treated him so kindly, instead of blasting him from the face of the earth, as he obviously deserved.

It is possible to regard Paul's conversion as some sort of psychological hallucination or seizure. It was certainly psychological in the sense that Paul's mind was very disturbed by what happened. People have speculated about the possible causes of the experience: was Paul, despite his ferociousness, feeling guilty about what he was doing? Had he been impressed by the Christians he had met and debated with? In particular there was Stephen, one of the earliest Christians to be killed for his faith; Paul was present at his lynching. Was he suppressing things, and did he now snap? Some of these possibilities are very likely. But whether his conversion is explained in such terms, or more simply in terms of a divine intervention, there is little question about what he thought had happened, and little question about its actual and dramatic effect.

The effect of Paul's conversion

Paul's conversion was an amazingly positive experience for the Christian community that he had been terrorizing, and a very negative experience for the Jewish authorities, who saw it as betrayal.

For Paul conversion marked the beginning of a very different life from his former one: he was no longer a champion of Jewish fundamentalism, indeed he became a hugely hated figure in the eyes of many of his Jewish former brothers and sisters. He became, unsurprisingly, a fervent advocate of the new Christian way, but he was not easily accepted by other Christians. Acts describes Ananias being very cautious about baptizing him; and when, after a year or more, he went to Jerusalem, the leaders of the church there remained suspicious and took considerable persuasion that he was genuinely a convert and safe to trust.[8]

It is worth saying that Paul never became part of the leadership of the Jerusalem church – the fact that the Jews of Jerusalem hated him would have made that impossible – but the Jewish Christians themselves seem to have had mixed feelings about him. This was not just because of his past as a persecutor, but also because he eventually became a champion of the liberal wing of the Christian church, which reached out into the Gentile world and moved away from its Jewish roots.

After his conversion Paul became an itinerant missionary around the Mediterranean world. He travelled hundreds of miles on foot, working as a tent-maker to support himself and facing all sorts of dangers, including four shipwrecks;[9] he founded churches, often in face of violent opposition from Jews and others; he wrote letters, which now make up a significant part of the Christian New Testament, to the churches that he founded; he was arrested on several occasions, imprisoned, beaten, and, according to very early evidence, finally executed in Rome.

Did Paul's ideas about Jesus as the Son of God come out of his conversion experience?

There seems little reason to question the main outlines of the story of Paul's conversion as we find it in the New Testament, not least because it is so unflattering to Paul. But what relevance does it have to the question of whether Paul was responsible for introducing ideas into Christianity that would become part of Christian orthodoxy, such as the idea that Jesus was divine and the Son of God? Some people believe that his mystical experience on the Damascus road led him to concoct or imagine these things.

Paul's conversion experience was certainly decisively important in persuading him that Jesus was divine (in some sense). The account of the event in the book of Acts (quoted above) says that immediately after his conversion he was preaching in the synagogues of Damascus and saying that "*He is the Son of God*".[10] In his letter to the Galatians Paul describes his conversion as God "revealing *his Son* to me".[11] In the same context he speaks of his "gospel", in other words his version of the Christian message, as coming to him "*through a revelation* of Jesus Christ".[12]

It is easy to see these three references as evidence that Paul's conversion was the thing that persuaded him of the divinity of Jesus. But it does not follow that the idea came to him first in his conversion experience, let alone that he was responsible for introducing the idea to other Christians.

This view seems unlikely for a whole variety of reasons.

1. His conversion brought him into a pre-existing group.
The church was a fast-growing movement before Paul's conversion, which is precisely why he had been persecuting it! It was successful because of its convictions about Jesus, notably about his resurrection from the dead. Paul became convinced of this himself on the Damascus road, but it was not his idea. What happened on the Damascus road was that he discovered the truth of what he had been opposing. Paul himself comments that people in Judea were saying: "He who used to persecute us is now preaching the faith he once tried to destroy."[13]

2. He was an outsider without influence in the early days of the church.
It might just be possible to argue that the early Christians had come to the conviction that Jesus was alive and risen from the dead, but that it was Paul who went on to conclude that he was divine. But this speculation has no basis to it. The fact that Paul was an outsider without influence in the Christian church for years after his conversion tells strongly against it.

Today we may think of Paul as an important and

influential figure. But all the evidence is that he was initially regarded by many other Christians with suspicion. He spent very little time in Jerusalem (as is clear from Acts and his letters), and he had no part in the leadership of the church in the earliest days. Had he wanted to propound revolutionary new ideas, it is not obvious that he would have been able to do so.

It is worth adding that Paul's conversion probably took place just two or three years after the lifetime of Jesus, when the stories and sayings of Jesus were very well known; for him to have "changed the story" in hugely significant ways would not have been so easy, even if he had been in a position to do so.

3. As a humble convert Paul would not have "changed" the religion of Jesus and the early Christians.
Paul's conversion experience was a hugely humbling one. In one of his letters he describes himself as the worst of sinners;[14] after all could there be a worse sin for a Jew than persecuting the messiah? His conversion was a physically, emotionally, and spiritually shattering experience for someone who had been so zealous in his former views, and so arrogant and ferocious in imposing them on others. This was hardly a basis for Paul to make radical changes to his new religion.

4. As a grateful convert Paul would not have wanted to change the religion he had discovered.
On the Damascus road Paul discovered astonishing mercy: the arch-persecutor of Christians was "saved" by Jesus. He discovered totally undeserved forgiveness and love. Paul

uses the word "grace" to describe this experience, and grace, and gratitude, are key themes in Paul's letters. He came to see the crucifixion of Jesus as the supreme expression of God's grace. Such emphases hardly go with the suggestion that Paul will have felt free to rewrite and reinvent the story and the religion of Jesus.

Paul's experience brought him into a personal, loving relationship with Jesus as his Lord which was unlike anything he had experienced in his relationship with God before, despite all his theological education. The evidence points to his becoming a humble devotee: he speaks of himself as "a slave of Jesus Christ", and of his supreme desire to know Christ better and to serve him faithfully.[15] There is every reason to take these professions of loyalty at their face value and to suppose that Paul will have been keen to be faithful to what he knew about Jesus, not to upstage or misrepresent him.

5. The conversion was a formative event for Paul, but not the source of Christian ideas of Jesus.
There is no denying the formative nature of his conversion for Paul himself; but there is no evidence to support the view that it led the Christian church to radically new views of Jesus.

Through his dramatic experience Paul unlearned various things:

• His former belief that Jesus was a false prophet who had deserved to be executed was turned upside down.

• His zealousness for the Jewish law was shaken radically.

• His aversion to "sinners" and Gentiles was undermined.

- So was his confidence in his own righteousness.
- He was no longer ready to persecute others violently.

Instead he discovered:

- Jesus was amazingly and divinely alive.
- He, Paul, was a major sinner.
- His unmerited conversion was a call to take the love of God to Gentile sinners.
- His new mission was to follow his master Jesus in the way of self-sacrifice (a total contrast to his previous, and vicious, mission, in which he attempted to impose his views by force).

This was a major revolution for Paul, but there is no evidence that his views about Jesus were seen by other Christians as controversial or novel. He just discovered what they already believed – by a sort of supernatural shortcut.

In conclusion

The view that Paul's conversion was a mystical experience leading him to novel interpretations of Jesus which he then introduced to the Christian church may seem initially plausible, but is in fact very unlikely to be justified. The revelation he received was not something novel, but was a heavenly endorsement of the views that he had previously bitterly opposed but now started to preach.

CHAPTER 4

Was Paul Interested in the Real Jesus? Evidence from Corinth on the Crucifixion and Resurrection

Paul's silence

Paul may have been devoted to Jesus after his conversion – a "slave of Jesus", as he says. But why then does he refer so little to Jesus' life and teaching in his letters? His failure to quote Jesus and to retell the stories of Jesus is one of the main arguments for the view that Paul was a religious innovator with his own ideas, rather than a faithful follower of Jesus.

According to the four gospels Jesus was a great teacher – his Sermon on the Mount is famous, with its teaching about turning the other cheek and loving one's enemies; his parables are now among the best-known stories in the world. But in none of his letters does Paul show any obvious knowledge of, or apparent interest in, those stories.

He talks about some of the same subjects as Jesus, for example about attitudes to money and to wealth, but he never says "remember what Jesus said about not laying up treasures on earth". Instead he gives his own views and opinions. And then there are all the miracles of Jesus: if the gospels are to be believed, Jesus was an important healer, and did other extraordinary things. But Paul is silent about these miracles.

This evidence is potentially very embarrassing to Christians. If St Paul either did not know these stories of Jesus or was not interested in them, what does this say? If the earliest Christian writings, the letters of Paul, ignore the stories of Jesus that we find in the gospels, what does this say? Perhaps that there never was a Jesus such as we find in the gospels; the real Jesus of Nazareth was a relatively ordinary Jewish prophet, whom Paul and others turned into a divine being. In any case Paul's silence about Jesus' life and teaching may seem to support the view that Paul was not interested in the real Jesus, but only in his own religious experience and imagination.

But is it true that Paul shows no significant knowledge of Jesus' life and ministry, as the gospels describe it? Despite initial impressions the answer is a resounding no. Let us investigate some of the evidence.

The real crucifixion

The first thing to say is that no one can doubt the importance to Paul of the death and resurrection of Jesus. They are everywhere in his letters, and are at the heart of what he believes and wants to say. Of course, the idea of Jesus being alive and not dead came to Paul through his Damascus road experience, and it is possible to argue that this idea, which is so important to Paul, has little to do with the real Jesus of history but everything to do with Paul's own theological imagination. Maybe it was also influenced by the Greek mystery religions, which were around in the world of Paul's day; these religions offered eternal life and told stories about the gods, death, and life.

But this explanation will not do. When Paul refers to the death of Jesus he is not thinking in generic religious terms of a god dying and rising; he is thinking of Jesus being crucified by the Romans outside Jerusalem. Crucifixion in Jesus' world was an agonizing and sordid form of public execution, a horrible, down-to-earth reality. No mystery religion had a god or hero being crucified at the heart of its mythology, or indeed anything that comes close to the Christian story. Jesus' crucifixion does not come out of such religions, but out of the historical context of first-century Palestine, where crucifixions were a gruesome reality.

The Romans and their allies used crucifixion when they wanted particularly to torture and punish people; its use is amply attested, not just in the Bible but in Jewish and Roman writings, and in archaeological finds. The bones of a crucified young man were recently found in Palestine together with the nails that were hammered through his wrists and through the ankles of his twisted legs to fix him to the cross. He was executed around the time of Jesus. There can be no doubt that Jesus was similarly crucified: the fact is attested by non-Christian sources, notably by the

Roman historian Tacitus. And it is not something that the Christians would have invented: who would imagine or want to imagine their leader being killed in such a way?

So the idea of Jesus being crucified, which was one of the major ingredients in Paul's theological thinking, is undoubted historical fact, not a strange mystical idea.

The story of the crucifixion and the events leading up to it

But did Paul simply know the fact that Jesus was crucified, or did he know anything more? One possible view is that he did know the fact, but he then imagined all kinds of things about the fact. It is possible that he did not have – and/or was not interested in – details about Jesus' death, but only thought about the general concept of death and resurrection. But this view is contradicted by the evidence, most notably by Paul's first letter to the Corinthians, where he says: "I received from the Lord what I also passed on to you that the Lord Jesus on the night he was betrayed took bread, and when he had given thanks he broke it, and said 'This is my body…'" He goes on to speak of Jesus giving his disciples a cup of wine and linking it with "my blood".[1]

This is the famous story of Jesus' Last Supper with his friends, and it shows that Paul knew not just that Jesus was crucified but at least some of the details of what happened. It is as though he starts quoting from the story of Jesus' crucifixion and of what led up to it as we find it in the gospels.

Against this view, some scholars have proposed that Paul invented the story of the last supper as we now have it and is the real originator of the Christian ritual meal that has been celebrated throughout the centuries (known variously as the "Lord's supper", the "Eucharist", "Holy Communion" or the "Mass"). Proponents of this view have observed that ceremonial meals featured in the so-called mystery religions, and have suggested that Paul drew on this tradition.

But this is a wholly implausible suggestion. The gospels describe the supper as a Passover meal of some kind shared by Jesus with his disciples in Jerusalem, just before his arrest and crucifixion. This account makes excellent historical sense. Passover was (and still is in the twenty-first century) a thoroughly Jewish festival. In Jesus' time it was the greatest Jewish festival of all, with huge numbers of pilgrims coming to Jerusalem to celebrate their national liberation from Egypt in the second millennium BC. It was also a very sensitive time for the Jewish and Roman authorities. The gospels' account of Jesus coming up to Jerusalem for the festival and eating with his friends fits perfectly into this context, as does their account of his arrest and execution by the Romans. So does the description of Jesus, the great teller of parables – pictures in words – giving his followers an acted parable involving bread and wine. The account is thoroughly plausible, and is a long away – geographically, theologically, and psychologically – from the mythical, mystical world of the mystery religions.

Paul admittedly does not make the connection explicit between the supper and Passover, but he does very explicitly associate Jesus and his death with Passover.[2] And there is no good reason to doubt that he knew and, as he said, had "received" the story of the Last Supper in something like the form we find it in the gospels.

There is further, though less direct, evidence elsewhere in Paul's letters that he knew and passed on to others the story of Jesus' death. In his letter to the Galatians he reminds them of the time when they became Christians, and he says "before your eyes Jesus Christ was publicly portrayed as crucified."[3] It is not completely clear what Paul means here, but it is probable that Paul is referring to how he and others explained the Christian good news to the Galatians. They did not just tell the Galatians that Jesus was crucified, with no explanation; rather they described, or portrayed, the crucifixion of Jesus. This is, of course, precisely what the gospels do, though people have often commented on how restrained they are in their description of such a gory event. (Modern retellings such as Mel Gibson's film *The Passion of the Christ*, by contrast, often portray the death of Jesus in horribly realistic detail.)

Later in the letter to the Galatians, Paul, who has been responding to some of his critics, says "From now on let no one cause me trouble, for I bear on my body the marks of Jesus."[4] Again it is not completely clear what Paul means, but most probably he is referring to scars on his body from the beatings he has experienced in the course of his mission, and associating these scars with the wounds of Jesus' crucifixion. Paul knew the story, and so did others, so he could allude to it in this way.

The story of Jesus' resurrection

If Paul knew of the events leading up to and including Jesus' crucifixion, he also knew the story or stories of what followed. So in his first letter to the Corinthians, he not only refers to the Last Supper as something that he "received" and "passed on" to them, but also says a little later "I passed on to you as of first importance what I also received that Christ died... was buried... was raised on the third day... and that he was seen [appeared]..."

Paul then gives a list of people to whom Christ appeared:

• Cephas (the Aramaic name for Peter),

• the twelve apostles,

• a group of more than 500 Christians,

• James,

• all the apostles.

He adds, "last of all, as to one born out of the right time, he appeared also to me. For I am the least of the apostles, unworthy to be called an apostle, because I persecuted the church of God."[5]

Paul on the resurrection of Jesus

For what I received I passed on to you as of first importance:
that Christ died for our sins according to the Scriptures, that he
was buried, that he was raised on the third day according to the
Scriptures, and that he appeared to Peter, and then to the Twelve.
After that, he appeared to more than five hundred of the brothers at
the same time, most of whom are still living, though some have fallen

asleep. Then he appeared to James, then to all the apostles, and last
of all he appeared to me also, as to one abnormally born.

I Corinthians 15:3–8

So Paul knows the stories of the burial of Jesus, of
his resurrection from the dead, and of his subsequent
appearances to various people. This is exactly how the four
gospels end their accounts of Jesus' life and ministry.

Paul's list of appearances does not correspond exactly
with those referred to in the gospels: there is some overlap,
since Luke's Gospel, for example, refers to Jesus' appearing
to Peter and to the Twelve. But there are some differences.
For example, Paul shows no knowledge of the gospels'
story of the women discovering the empty tomb. And he
includes himself in the list of those who saw Jesus. Some
people argue from these differences that Paul contradicts
the gospels' account. They also suggest that his inclusion of
himself in the list of those who saw the risen Jesus shows
that he did not accept the gospels' picture of Jesus' body
physically coming to life again and leaving the tomb where it
was buried.

However, these arguments are not convincing: the clear
implication of Paul's words about Jesus being buried and
then "raised" is that his physical body was raised from the
place where he was buried. Paul's failure to mention the
women proves nothing; he is being selective in his account.
And his reference to his own extraordinary Damascus road
experience in no way indicates that he thought that all the
appearances were visionary. It may rather be that Paul saw
Jesus' appearance to him as something more than a vision;

but in any case he quite clearly puts his own "seeing" of Jesus into a special category, as different from the others.

Whatever we may think about the New Testament claims that Jesus rose from the dead and appeared to people – some have regarded the appearances as hallucinations – it is clear that Paul knew something like the stories that we find in the gospels. And it would be very difficult to make a case for Paul being the originator of the idea of the resurrection: he refers to other very well-known people, who were not his protégés, who were alive when he was writing, whom he had met, and who claimed to have seen the risen Jesus.

Some important points

The significance of the evidence of Paul's first letter to the Corinthians can hardly be over-emphasized. A number of points are important:

1. We know when 1 Corinthians was written

First, we can date the letter with confidence to AD 55 (plus or minus a year or two) through a comparison of this and other New Testament documents with other ancient historical sources. In particular:

- The inscription noted earlier refers to a Roman called Gallio being governor of Corinth in AD 51–52.

- The book of Acts reports that Paul was in Corinth in the time of Gallio, and that he was indeed brought before the governor by his opponents.

- It also says that Paul stayed in Corinth with a couple

who became very good friends of his, named Aquila and Priscilla, who had come to Corinth as a result of the expulsion of the Jews from Rome in AD 49.

• This expulsion is referred to by the Roman historian Suetonius, who was not a Christian.[6]

All of this enables us to date Paul's founding of the church in Corinth to AD 50–52; and then the contents of the letter enable us to date his first letter to the Corinthians to about three years later. It was clearly written just a few years after Paul had been there, to deal with various problems that had arisen.

It is worth adding that there is no reasonable doubt about 1 Corinthians being a genuine letter of Paul. Questions have been raised about the authorship of some of the so-called Pauline letters. But 1 Corinthians, like Galatians, is almost universally regarded as genuine. It shows a church with a whole host of problems, which neither Paul nor an admirer of Paul could or would have invented. Among other things:

• The church was squabbling over its leaders.

• It had some with very "advanced" ethical views, with some arguing that Christians could have sex with prostitutes while others were arguing that they should be celibate.

• Some people were flirting dangerously with the idolatry of the pagan world.

• Some were concerned over gender issues.

• Their services (held in homes, not in a church building) were chaotic.

The Corinthian Christians had multiple problems, and Paul's first letter to them is a thoroughly credible response.

2. Not fuzzy memories, but careful recollection of traditions

An emphasis on passing on traditions emerges from the letter and from the other evidence. We are not sure when the gospels were written down, but most people think that it was between AD 60 and AD 90. As we saw earlier, a fragment of John's Gospel was found in Egypt around 1920 which has been dated by experts in ancient manuscripts to about AD 125. So the gospels were written before then, and certainly in some cases long before then. Acts was written by a companion of Paul – hence the "we" passages – and that means that Luke's Gospel, the volume that preceded Acts, will have been written perhaps as early as the AD 60s.

But how were the stories of Jesus preserved before they achieved written form? The answer is that they will have been passed down orally from person to person. This could sound alarming to those of us brought up in literary cultures, in which we memorize very little and very inaccurately. However, in non-literary cultures or semi-literary cultures memorization is typically very accurate and very important; this was certainly true in the Jewish world of Jesus, where the teaching of the rabbis was learned and transmitted extensively and with great accuracy.

Did the Christians pass down their traditions with similar care? Some scholars have doubted it. But Paul's evidence is that the passing on of the stories of Jesus was something important: he says both of the Last Supper and of the resurrection that "I passed down what I also received", and he was himself trained in the Jewish traditions.

Paul received much "by revelation" through his Damascus road experience. It might be argued that he also received the stories of the Last Supper and the resurrection appearances in the same way – by direct revelation from the Lord. But the similarity to the gospel traditions, and the fact that he speaks in the same breath of "passing on" what he received to others, strongly suggests that Paul received these traditions in the same way that he passed them on – from other Christians who told him the good news of Jesus when he became a Christian himself.

Paul discovered Jesus in a life-transforming way on the Damascus road, but he did not learn all he knew about Jesus directly from Jesus. He knew something about Jesus even when he was persecuting Christians and disputing with them, and after his conversion he learned from those who had been Christians before him. He was not an inventor of traditions but a receiver, right back in the AD 30s when he was converted.

3. The content of Paul's teaching about Jesus

Paul also passed traditions on to others. The impression that Paul made up a lot of the Christian gospel is not supported by the evidence. He passed on the stories of Jesus and, according to 1 Corinthians 15, this was "the gospel that I proclaimed to you". Sometimes people are very unimaginative in their view of what Paul preached and taught about Jesus when he journeyed round the Mediterranean world. He did not tell people only about the possibility of a mystical experience such as he himself had on the Damascus road; he gave them a message about Jesus being crucified outside Jerusalem and then raised to life. In other words, he passed on the story of Jesus.

And it is wholly unlikely that he simply referred to Jesus' dying and rising without giving any other information about the Lord's life and teaching. People would have asked for more information, and he would certainly have told them much more about the story of Jesus and its importance. The evidence points in the same direction as what makes sense: Paul did not invent a new religion based on the mystery religions or his own mystical experience, he passed on the kinds of tradition about Jesus that we find in the gospels.

4. Paul the trouble-shooter

But why do we find so few of these traditions in Paul's letters? The reason that Paul referred to the traditions of Jesus' Last Supper and to the resurrection in 1 Corinthians is because he was dealing in this letter with problems in the Corinthian church.

He wrote about the Last Supper because of the disorder in the Lord's Supper meals that took place each week in the Christian community in Corinth: there was a division between rich and poor Christians, with the rich being very well fed and the poor getting little. Paul was outraged at this, and so in his letter he reminded the Corinthians of the origins of the supper and of its meaning.[7]

The Corinthians also had issues over life after death, with some of them questioning the idea of resurrection. Probably influenced by Greek ideas of the immortality of the soul, they were questioning whether people's bodies would also be raised. In this context Paul reminded them of the good news that he had preached, and how it included the bodily resurrection of Jesus as an important element. He listed the resurrection appearances of Jesus to emphasize the point. Here, as with the Last Supper, Paul recalled parts of the story of Jesus in order to deal with particular problems that the Corinthians had. His letter to them is, more than anything else, a trouble-shooting letter.

This is typical of Paul's letters: they are what scholars have called "occasional", responding to questions and problems that have arisen at a particular time in the place to which he is writing. So the fact that he recalls the Last Supper and the resurrection appearances but not other things from Jesus' life and ministry does not prove that he does not know anything else. He has no need to refer, for example, to Jesus' parable of the Good Samaritan or to the gospel story about Jesus being tempted and tested by the devil in the wilderness.

It is important to appreciate that Paul's silence does not prove his ignorance. If the Corinthians had not had problems with their Lord's Supper meal, or if we did not have the text of 1 Corinthians, we would have no evidence at all to indicate that Paul knew or cared about the Lord's Supper. In fact it was important to him; his churches had the Supper together each week, in obedience to the instructions of Jesus himself. So Paul's silence on this matter in his letters to the Thessalonians and the Philippians (churches he founded at the same time as he founded the church in Corinth) does not prove that he failed to pass on that teaching in those places: there is no doubt that he did.

The conclusion that Paul's reticence in quoting traditions about Jesus indicates a lack of interest or knowledge is simply wrong. Indeed the truth may be exactly the opposite: the evidence is that Paul passed traditions of Jesus on to others when he first evangelized them. So it was something that happened when he first founded a church rather than in his subsequent letters, which were very much follow-up documents. The churches already had the traditions of Jesus, passed on to them by Paul, and he did not need to repeat them. He only had to remind the churches occasionally if something in the situation called for such a reminder, as it did with the Last Supper and with the resurrection.

Paul's silence about the ministry of Jesus paradoxically suggests its importance for him, and tells against the view that he was in the habit of innovatively retelling the story of Jesus. The evidence points to him passing on received traditions about Jesus and regarding them as of foundational importance.

Despite this important argument, there might well be lingering questions if Paul were wholly silent about Jesus except for the references to the Last Supper and the resurrection. It could have been that he had traditions of the passion and resurrection of Jesus, perhaps liturgically preserved – used in the worship and rituals of the early church – but that he had no other traditions and was really not interested in anything else to do with Jesus. This would arguably seem a little odd. And the next set of evidence to be examined points to his wider knowledge of and interest in Jesus.

CHAPTER 5

Sex, Apostleship, and Love: More Evidence from Corinth and Beyond

The clearest evidence for Paul knowing about the death and resurrection of Jesus comes from his first letter to the Corinthians; and that letter also shows that he knows other parts of the story of Jesus, in particular Jesus' teaching.

Paul on marriage: evidence in 1 Corinthians

The Corinthians' issues about sex and Paul's reply

The most obvious example of this is in chapter 7 of first Corinthians, where Paul is discussing questions of marriage and singleness. Some of the Corinthians seem to have been arguing that really spiritual people should abstain from sex. This may sound odd now, but it makes sense in terms of the following facts:

- The Corinthians were religiously zealous, and very interested in spiritual experiences.

- They were expecting Jesus to come back to the world again soon, having gone to heaven shortly after his death.

- In the Greek world of the time there was plenty of promiscuity and sexual licence.

- Some Greeks had a negative view of the body as something unimportant and temporary rather than spiritual and eternal.

So the conclusion of some of the Christians in Corinth was that real spirituality entails celibacy, and even that married people should terminate their marriages.

Paul did not accept this logic. He was single himself, and he agreed that singleness has real advantages for the committed Christian, since marriage and family life necessarily bring complications and distractions into people's lives. Paul himself could not have had the remarkable ministry that he did if he had needed to care for a family. However, although Paul could wish for more people to be in his position, he was quite clear that singleness is not everyone's calling. "Each has their own gift from God, one in this way, one in that way," he says, and each should live according to the Lord's calling.[1]

Paul's appeal to Jesus

As for the idea that married Christians should stop having sex together, Paul is completely opposed to that. Do not deprive one another, he says to married couples. The one exception he allows is when the couple both agree on a temporary period of sexual fasting in the context of prayer, and he insists that it should be temporary.[2]

The idea that married couples should abandon their marriages altogether is out of the question for Paul, and it is in this context that he quotes Jesus' teaching. He says: "To the married I give this command (not I, but the Lord): the wife should not separate from her husband. But if she does, she must remain unmarried or else be reconciled to her husband. And a husband must not divorce his wife."[3]

Paul is clearly quoting here from Jesus' teaching about marriage and divorce, that we find in Matthew's and Mark's Gospels. This is evident first from the way Paul introduces the teaching concerned with the words "not I, *but the Lord*". These words function rather like quotation marks at the beginning, and then he marks the end of the quotation when he introduces the next section: "but to the rest I say (I *not the Lord*)…"[4]

It is evident secondly because of the similarity between the ideas in the first letter to the Corinthians and those in Matthew and Mark. In the first letter to the Corinthians there is:

• a general statement about not separating or divorcing, then;

• a "but if" clause saying that, if there is a separation, the couple should remain unmarried or be reconciled.

In Mark chapter 10, when Jesus is asked about divorce, his reply comes in two stages:

• a general statement "What then God has joined, let no human being separate." Then

• a "but whoever" statement specifically saying that remarriage is adulterous. "Whoever divorces his wife and marries another woman commits adultery against her. And if she divorces her husband and marries another man, she commits adultery."[5]

The sequence of ideas, as well as the ideas themselves, is very similar.

And so, thirdly, is some of the wording, most notably the use of the verb "to separate".

The conclusion from this and from other evidence (for example the fact that Jesus and Paul both speak about the Genesis story of God creating man and woman) is that Paul is using Jesus' teaching to refute the Corinthian ascetics with their extreme ideas about sexual abstinence.

Paul's intelligent use of Jesus' teaching

There are a number of other interesting points to come out of this comparison.

The first is that Paul regards the teaching of Jesus as relevant and even decisive for the issue that he is discussing.

The second is that he is using Jesus' teaching flexibly. Paul's issue is to do with singleness and Corinthian ascetics; Jesus' issue was a question from his opponents about his view on divorce. Paul is not so rigid as simply to say that Jesus did not address the Corinthians' question about of spirituality and singleness; he is flexible enough to apply Jesus' teaching in one context to a different one.

The third point is related: Paul is "quoting" Jesus here, but it is more of a paraphrase than a quotation as such. The teaching is recognizably that found in Mark chapter 10 and yet, whereas Jesus spoke first of the man divorcing his wife, Paul speaks first of the wife wanting to separate from her husband. A plausible explanation for this is that it was women in the Corinthian church who were pressing most for celibacy; it could have seemed a very attractive spirituality in a society where women were very much tied to home and to child-bearing. Whether or not this is the case, the impression given is of the teaching of Jesus being authoritative for Paul, and applicable to different situations.

But does Paul not ignore Jesus' teaching?

There is a possible counter-argument to this, however, in that when Paul goes on to the next question in chapter 7 he seems to be giving less authority to Jesus' teaching. The question is: what about married Christians who have unconverted partners? Should they separate? The argument for separation probably seemed rather strong: the Christians felt that they had been made "holy" or "clean" by God when they came to faith and were baptized, but their unconverted partners, and perhaps their children, were still unholy. Was it religiously defiling to remain in such a relationship?

Paul rejects this view, arguing exactly the opposite: he says that the holiness of the Christian partner makes the marriage relationship holy, and this holiness extends to the non-Christian partner and the children. So they should not separate. However, Paul does allow that, if the non-Christian partner takes the initiative and demands a separation, then the Christian "is not bound... for God has called you to peace."[6] It is here that Paul is seen by some as preferring his own view to that of Jesus.

However, this reading of Paul is unjustified: first, because Paul says explicitly that Jesus had not pronounced specifically on this matter, so he is having to give his own view (v.12). Secondly, Paul still gives weight to Jesus' teaching, arguing that the Christian should, if possible, not divorce. Paul knew and valued the teaching of Jesus on marriage and divorce, and he saw the teaching of Jesus as key to addressing such important issues.

Some people have argued that the gospel writers got their ideas from Paul, rather than Paul getting his from Jesus. After all, Paul's letters were written before the gospels. However, the evidence of this and other cases suggests that this is not likely. Here Paul's use of "not I but the Lord" shows that he is quoting Jesus. And in any case it is wholly improbable that Paul's teaching on singleness in his letter to the Corinthians could have generated the gospel accounts of Jesus being asked about divorce. Those accounts make excellent sense in Jesus' Galilean context: divorce was a controversial issue among rabbis, with some taking a strict line and prohibiting divorce except for adultery, and others allowing divorce on demand (though only for husbands). Divorce was also a controversial issue in Galilean society more widely following the scandalous divorces and remarriage of Herod, the ruler of Galilee, and his second wife, Herodias. There is no reasonable doubt that Paul got his teaching from Jesus.

Paul on apostleship: evidence from 1 Corinthians 9

Much the same may be said about Paul's remarks on Christian ministry, also in his first letter to the Corinthians. He quotes Jesus as follows: "So also the Lord instructed that those who proclaim the gospel should get their living from the gospel."[7] This is widely recognized as a reference to Jesus' words to his disciples when he sent them out on mission. Jesus told them that they need not take equipment or provisions with them, and commented that "The labourer is worthy of his pay/reward."[8]

As with Paul's use of Jesus' teaching on divorce, this is a paraphrase, not a word-for-word quotation of what Jesus said. But it is clear that Paul is referring to this particular saying of Jesus:

- from the fact that Paul says "so also the Lord instructed";

- from the fact that what Paul and Jesus say about the Christian minister being rewarded is so similar;

- from the broader parallels between Paul's teaching in this part of 1 Corinthians and Jesus' instructions to his disciples as they are recorded in the gospels. The gospels record Jesus sending out the apostles, giving them "authority", and telling them to accept food, drink, and hospitality on their mission, for "the labourer is worthy of his pay/reward". In 1 Corinthians 9 Paul starts by talking about himself and the apostles; and he speaks of his "authority" and his right to food and drink. He reflects at length about his "pay/reward".

The similarities are such as to make it, once again, very probable that Paul is using and reflecting on the Lord's teaching and words.

But does Paul really care about what Jesus said?

In this case Paul seems to quote the Lord's words only to justify his own disobedience to them, since Paul's policy was *not* to accept the support of those to whom he went in mission. He earned his own living by tent-making rather than taking anything from those among whom he worked.

It is not very difficult to read between the lines of what Paul says here, and to see one of the accusations made against Paul by his opponents: "You, Paul, claim to be an apostle of Jesus, but you are flagrantly and proudly ignoring Jesus' instructions to the apostles whom he sent out."

This seems a likely background to Paul's teaching in this part of his letter to the Corinthians. But does it prove that Paul preferred his own opinions to those of Jesus? Paul would undoubtedly deny it, and chapter 9 of the letter is his explanation:

• He agrees that Jesus spoke of gospel-ministers being supported in their ministry.

• He says that this was a right that he, Paul, could legitimately have claimed for himself.

• However, he has chosen to forgo that right "rather than put an obstacle in the way of the gospel of Christ".[9]

He goes on to say that he chose to "present the gospel free of charge", not taking up his rights, and he speaks of "making himself a slave of all" to win them for Christ.[10] All of this is said in the context of Paul's main concern in chapter 9, which is to encourage the Corinthians not to insist on their rights, but to be willing to give them up for others.

To see Paul's argument as setting aside Jesus' teaching in favour of his own opinion is to insist on a very literalistic and wooden interpretation of Jesus' words, which is exactly what his critics were doing. Jesus' words to the disciples going out on local missions in Palestine and urging them to travel light and to accept local hospitality gratefully were important: he did not want them to go elaborately equipped or heavily weighed down. But to say that therefore Paul should just have accepted the hospitality of his friends Aquila and Priscilla, or of other people in Corinth, and that he should not have contributed to his living expenses by joining them in their tent-making business is absurd.

Paul probably considered that living off a wealthy patron in Corinth, as some other philosophical and religious teachers did, would have been quite undesirable; it would have sent out exactly the wrong signal from a servant of Jesus who gave of himself freely. Charging for his teaching or begging – two other options for teachers in Paul's world – would have been even more unthinkable. Working as a tent-maker with Aquila and Priscilla, on the other hand, would be arduous, but would send out the right signals for someone trying to model his life on Jesus. And Paul may also have calculated that being a tent-maker and leather worker would give him openings in the bazaar to talk to fellow workers, customers, and passers-by.

In 1 Corinthians 9 Paul is not questioning the validity of the teaching of Jesus that he quotes or preferring his own views to those of Jesus. He quotes the teaching of Jesus, explains it, and stands by it. But he interprets it intelligently, not woodenly, and in a way entirely in keeping with Jesus' own teaching and attitudes. It is interesting to realize that both Paul's critics and Paul himself were quoting from Jesus and arguing about the meaning and applicability of his teaching. Jesus' teaching, including his teaching on divorce and marriage and his instructions to his disciples on apostolic mission, was well known and important.

Loving and serving

In justifying his policy of working to earn his living, Paul spoke, as we saw, of "making myself *a slave of all*". This striking phrase is very likely to be an echo of Jesus' teaching to his disciples on another occasion. This is described in Mark's Gospel: the disciples were arguing about their positions in Jesus' coming kingdom, and Jesus responded by contrasting worldly authority and leadership with the way of serving that should characterize his disciples, and said: "Whoever wants to become great among you must be your servant, and whoever wants to be first must be *slave of all*." Jesus went on to speak of himself as one who came not to be served but to serve and to give his life for others.[11]

The argument that Paul is drawing on Jesus' teaching when he speaks of being a "slave to all" is not just based on the similarity of the words used in Jesus' teaching. Other considerations reinforce the case:

1. A strong emphasis on leaders being humble servants is characteristic of the gospel accounts of Jesus, notably in this story in Mark, but also at other points in the gospels. One of the most striking examples is in John's Gospel, where Jesus washes his disciples' feet. Washing the feet of dinner guests who had come in from the dusty streets was normally the task of a servant but, according to John's Gospel, Jesus did it for his disciples shortly before his death. They were shocked, but Jesus explained that he was setting them an example.[12]

2. This emphasis on serving, and on Jesus as the supreme servant, is echoed in many of Paul's letters, not just 1

Corinthians. One of the most famous passages in all of Paul's letters is in Philippians, where he speaks of Jesus as one who was "in the form of God", but who "emptied himself", taking the "form of servant" and finally going to death "even death on a cross". Paul could very easily have had in mind the story of Jesus washing his disciples' feet just before his crucifixion. The same theme comes out in Paul's letter to the Galatians, where he says: "through love be slaves to one another", and later, "carry each other's burdens, and so fulfil the law of Christ".[13] Serving and helping one another is specifically associated by Paul with Jesus.

3. Scholars have been puzzled by the phrase "the law of Christ" in the verse from Galatians. What does Paul mean by "the law of Christ" and why does he use that phrase?

Most scholars are agreed that for Paul the law of Christ is love, and this makes sense since love was central to both Jesus' teaching and Paul's. So far as Jesus is concerned, we only need to remember the parable of the Good Samaritan and the Sermon on the Mount, including the counterintuitive command to love one's enemies – "bless those who curse you", Jesus says. As for Paul, he comes very close to Jesus' words in his letter to the Romans when he says "bless those who persecute you; bless and do not curse them".[14] The primacy of love for Paul is illustrated in his famous "hymn" about love, so often quoted at weddings, that begins, "if I speak in the tongues of men and of angels but have not love, I am a noisy gong or a clanging cymbal..." and ends "So now faith, hope, and love abide, these three, but the greatest of these is love."[15] The agreement of Jesus and Paul in emphasizing love as the supreme ethical category is striking.

Nevertheless, why does Paul speak of the "law" of Christ? It could be that he is referring to the Old Testament command "love your neighbour as yourself", since that command was certainly important in Jesus' teaching and it was also important to Paul. However, would he have called that command "the law of Christ", since he knew very well that it was a law of Moses and not something original to Jesus?

A more likely explanation is suggested by the Gospel of John, where Jesus says to his disciples "A new commandment I give to you, that you should love one another, as I loved you that you also should love one another. By this shall all know that you are my disciples if you have love for one another."[16] Here "love one another" is specifically identified as Jesus' distinctive command. It is a command to his disciples about how they should relate within the Christian community, whereas "Love your neighbour" is something broader. This focused command fits excellently with Paul's words to the Galatians: "bear one another's burdens, and so fulfil *the law of Christ*."

A possible objection to this view is that only John's Gospel, usually seen as the last gospel to be written, identifies this as Jesus' distinctive command: why do the other gospels not mention it? But the difficulty evaporates when we note two things: first, in John the command to love one another follows the story of Jesus washing the disciples' feet, so loving one another is associated with humbly serving one another.[17] And secondly, in Mark Jesus tells his disciples that serving one another is to be their distinctive style of leadership. The same point is being made in slightly different words: the particular mark of Jesus' disciples is to be self-sacrificial love and service of one another. Paul puts the two together when he tells the Galatians "through love be slaves to one another". And when he refers to this as "the law of Christ" he traces it back to Jesus.

If this argument seems slightly complex, the essential point is very simple. Paul's strong emphases on love and humble service reflect the teaching and the example of Jesus. He tried to shape his own life accordingly, making himself the "slave of all", and he called others to live according to the "law" of Christ. One scholar has summed up Paul's theology in the word "cruciformity":[18] Paul saw the loving sacrifice of Jesus as at the heart of everything, and as his own inspiration. The Paul who worked hard as a tent-maker in order to commend Jesus to others had come a long way from his days as an arrogant young Pharisee, imposing his views on others by force. He had come a long way, too, from the ideals of the Greco-Roman world, where status, honour, and power were the things to which people aspired.

Conclusion

So was Paul really interested in Jesus, or only in his own religious ideas? The previous chapter looked at the heart of Paul's "gospel", the death and resurrection of Jesus, and showed how Paul was not a theological innovator, but someone who knew and made full use of the stories of Jesus. This chapter has shown how his teaching on ethical matters and on Christian ministry was similarly informed and inspired by Jesus' teaching. The next chapter will conclude the discussion of Paul's knowledge of Jesus, looking at some of Paul's teaching about Jesus himself.

CHAPTER 6

"Abba", and What Happens When We Die: Evidence from Galatia and Thessalonica

It would be possible simply to go on noting instances from Paul's first letter to the Corinthians. But instead I shall turn to Galatians, which may have been Paul's earliest letter, to observe one particularly striking piece of evidence.

Abba, Father

In chapter 4 of the letter Paul says: "when the fullness of time had come, God sent out his son, born of a woman, born under the law, so that he might liberate those under the law, so that we might receive adoption as sons. And because you are sons God sent the Spirit of his Son into our hearts crying, 'Abba, Father'."[1]

The most striking thing in these verses is the final phrase, "Abba, Father". Both here and in his letter to the Romans, where Paul speaks similarly of Christians receiving the Spirit of adoption as sons by whom we cry "Abba, Father", Paul drops without warning into Aramaic.[2] Aramaic was the common language of Palestine (related to Hebrew) and was probably the first language of Jesus and his followers. But in Galatians Paul is writing in Greek to people who speak Greek, not Aramaic. Why does he use this language when speaking of the work of the Holy Spirit in the hearts of Christian believers?

The obvious and only satisfactory answer is that this Aramaic word was associated with Jesus, who did speak Aramaic. This is also suggested by Mark's Gospel, which describes Jesus crying out "Abba" in the Garden of Gethsemane shortly before his death,[3] and by Paul's own words here: "God sent the Spirit *of his Son* into our hearts crying 'Abba, Father'."

It seems that this way of addressing God was distinctive to Jesus. Experts in ancient Judaism tell us that it was the family word for the father of the family (like the English "Daddy", or perhaps the more respectful "Papa"): Jews did not normally use it when addressing the holy God of Israel. Jesus, however, did so, and probably taught his disciples to do so; and this was so striking and revolutionary that the Aramaic word stayed in the Christian vocabulary, even when Christianity moved into the non-Aramaic-speaking world.

These passages are further strong evidence against the argument that the gospel writers got their ideas from Paul, rather than Paul getting his ideas from Jesus. It would be perverse to suggest that Paul came up with the idea of addressing God as "Abba", and that it then got ascribed to Jesus. On the other hand, it is entirely likely that Paul knew the story of Jesus in Gethsemane, just as he knew about the Last Supper and about the arrest and death of Jesus, and that hence he knew of Jesus' words.

The next chapter will return to the importance of Jesus' use of "Abba" for the big question of where Paul got the idea of Jesus' divinity. At this point all we need to note is that Paul was familiar with this significant usage.

Did Paul know about the virgin birth of Jesus?

Both Matthew and Luke describe – in quite different ways – Jesus being miraculously conceived and born of a virgin mother, Mary. Paul does not explicitly refer to this story. However, in the same passage in Galatians where he uses the word "Abba", he says:

> "When the fullness of time had come, God sent out his Son, born of a woman, born under the law, so that he might liberate those under the law…"
>
> Galatians 4:4

This is intriguingly reminiscent of Luke's story of the birth of Jesus, which:

- is full of excitement about the time of fulfilment having come;
- speaks of Jesus as "Son of the most high" and "Son of God";
- focuses its account on his mother, Mary;
- emphasizes Jesus being brought to Jerusalem to the temple for all that the Jewish law required;
- speaks of Jesus the liberator of Jerusalem and the Jews (Luke chapters 1 and 2).

It could well be that Paul has something like Luke's story in mind. It is interesting that he uses a different Greek word for Jesus' birth than for other normal births referred to in the letter (Galatians 4:23).

Verdict: it is possible, but the evidence is not conclusive.

Paul on Jesus coming back: evidence from 1 Thessalonians

If Galatians is Paul's earliest letter, the first letter to the Thessalonians comes quite a close second. And for those who give Galatians a later date, in the AD 50s, first Thessalonians is the earliest. It was probably written around AD 50.

Evidence for the date of the first letter to the Thessalonians

The evidence for this is:

(a) It was clearly written soon after Paul had been in Thessalonica founding the church there: in the highly autobiographical first three chapters he describes his anxiety since leaving the Thessalonians not long before.

(b) We know from the book of Acts that Paul moved on from Thessalonica in north Greece to Corinth in south Greece, and we know that he was in Corinth about AD 50 (see above, and Acts 17 and18). First Thessalonians was probably written when Paul was in Corinth.

Whereas Paul's first letter to the Corinthians addresses a whole range of problems that had arisen in Corinth since Paul was there – he had been away for several years – 1 Thessalonians focuses on one main problem that had arisen in the months since Paul was there, and it concerned the expected return of Jesus.

The early Christians believed that after his resurrection Jesus went to heaven: there is an account of his "ascension" in the book of Acts.[4] The Christians believed that he would return to them, probably sooner rather than later. First Corinthians uses an Aramaic expression, "Maranatha", at the very end of the letter, which means "Our Lord, come!".[5] We can infer from this that the very first Christians, who spoke Aramaic, used this mini-prayer to express their eager hope for Jesus' return.

The Thessalonian Christians were equally expectant. Paul describes their conversion at the start of his letter, and says "you turned to God from idols to serve the living and true God and to wait for his Son from heaven, whom he raised from the dead, Jesus..."[6] This hope was no doubt especially important to the Thessalonian Christians since they faced acute persecution (as we can see from Paul's letter to them and from the book of Acts); they were longing for their Lord to come back and rescue them and bring them into his kingdom. The clause in the Lord's Prayer "Your kingdom come" would have been full of relevance and meaning to them.

But what was their problem? Simply that some of the church members had died: Paul uses the language of "falling asleep".[7] The mortality of their spiritual brothers and sisters seems to have caused them much anxiety and grief, because they were afraid that their dead fellow-believers had missed out on the coming kingdom that Jesus was going to bring. This worry may seem as odd to us as the Corinthian idea that all Christians should abstain from sex; but it was not so odd in their context, since they were expecting Jesus imminently and at any time.

In Paul's response to their anxieties we find him referring to Jesus' own death and resurrection. Paul's argument is that, just as Jesus died and rose again, so his followers who had died would also rise again at the time of Jesus' coming. The Thessalonians should not worry. Paul then goes on to explain at some length what will happen when Jesus comes back, assuring the Thessalonians that Christians, dead and alive, will go to be with the Lord. He introduces this explanation with the words "for this we declare to you by a word from the Lord".[8]

This phrase has caused much soul searching among scholars: to what "word from the Lord" is Paul referring? The most plausible explanation is that this is another example (like those in his letter to the Corinthians) of Paul referring back to the teaching of Jesus, "the Lord".

This is confirmed by a comparison of what Paul goes on to say with teaching of Jesus as it is recorded in the gospels. Paul describes the return of Jesus, and there are many parallels with what Jesus says in Matthew's Gospel (chapters 24 and 25), and in Mark's and Luke's Gospels. Here are some of the most striking parallels.

In chapter 4 of first Thessalonians Paul speaks of:

• the Lord descending from heaven;

• the voice of an archangel;

• the sound of the trumpet of God;

• Christians who are alive being caught up together in the clouds to meet the Lord in the air.

In chapter 24 of Matthew Jesus speaks of:

• the Son of Man (that is, Jesus himself) coming "on the clouds of the sky";

- sending out his angels with a loud trumpet call;
- gathering the elect from the four winds;
- one person being taken and one left.

The pictures and imagery are very similar indeed.

In the next section of first Thessalonians Paul goes on to discuss the likely timing of the Lord's coming, and he says, interestingly, "we do not need to write to you, for you know very well that the day of the Lord will come like a thief in the night."[9] He goes on to talk about the suddenness of the Lord's coming, and of the need for Christians to "keep awake" for the Lord's return.

The interesting thief

Paul says that the Thessalonians are fully aware that the day of the Lord will come "like a thief", and that he does not need to write to tell them. The clear implication is that they have been taught this before. And this is explicable when we look back at Jesus' teaching in Matthew chapter 24, where Jesus says "keep watch, because you do not know on what day your Lord will come. But understand this: If the owner of the house had known at what time of night the thief was coming, he would have kept watch and would not have let his house be broken into. So you also must be ready, because the Son of Man will come at an hour when you do not expect him."[10]

This parable, in which Jesus compares his return to the coming of a thief because of its suddenness and unpredictability, is also found in Luke's Gospel, and it seems very probable indeed that Paul is referring back to it. It was part of the teaching of Jesus that had been passed on to the Thessalonians, which is why Paul can say that "you know very well".

Some people have suggested that the gospel writers might have got this parable from Paul rather than Paul getting it from Jesus. But this is entirely improbable, for at least two reasons.

First, it is totally unlikely that Paul or any other Christian would have come up with the comparison of Jesus to a thief: Jesus was their beloved Lord, not a criminal! However, if the comparison came from Jesus himself – and he could well have spoken in this way of himself without embarrassment in order to make his point about being ready for the unexpected – it would have been acceptable for Paul and other New Testament writers to echo his words.

Secondly, Paul indicates that the idea does at least predate the writing of his letter to the Thessalonians, because he says: "you know very well". And just a few verses before he has spoken about "a word from the Lord", which can plausibly be taken to mean that he is quoting Jesus' teaching in this part of his letter.

A problem: the Lord's lost word?

There is, however, a potential problem with the last part of this argument. Paul actually says that he has "a word from the Lord" when he is addressing the question of Christians who have died. But there is no saying of Jesus in the gospels which corresponds to this "word"; indeed the question of people dying before the Lord's return does not seem to arise in Jesus' teaching.

Paul could be referring to some teaching of Jesus that we do not have recorded in the gospels, as some scholars have speculated; others have suggested that he is referring to the word of a Christian prophet speaking in the name of Jesus.

However, we have seen when looking at Paul's use of Jesus' teaching in other contexts that he does not necessarily use Jesus' teaching in a very literalistic way; he applies it flexibly and intelligently to new questions – as in his discussion of singleness in his letter to the Corinthians. It seems likely that this is another such case. Paul could well have deduced that the Lord would save deceased Christians: the Lord who would come from heaven to gather his elect, taking one and leaving another, would surely raise his faithful followers who had "fallen asleep" to be with him.

The wise and foolish girls: a relevant word of the Lord

But it is likely that Paul had something more specific from Jesus' teaching in mind, since close to the parable of the thief in Matthew's Gospel is Jesus' parable of the wise and foolish girls. Ten girls are waiting for a wedding feast to begin. They are waiting for the bridegroom to arrive (in accordance with the customs of the time), but he is delayed until late at night, and they fall asleep as they wait. When there is a shout announcing his arrival, the five girls who are wise are ready to meet him and go into the wedding feast with him. But the five foolish girls have no oil for their lamps, and when they come to the feast late they are turned away.[11]

If Paul knew this parable, then he could well have seen it as speaking very directly to the Thessalonians' anxieties. They were worried about people dying before the Lord's return, and the parable was about the master coming later than expected, when the girls had fallen asleep.

The phrases used in the parable and in Paul's letter match each other in various ways – there are:

• the falling asleep of the faithful and of the girls;

• the "loud command" at the return of the Lord and the "cry" at the arrival of the bridegroom;

• the faithful meeting the Lord and the girls coming out to meet the bridegroom;

• the faithful being with the Lord and the girls being with the bridegroom at the feast.

The fit is very good: it seems that we have another example of Paul using the teaching of Jesus creatively to answer questions that had arisen.

Other parables

There is some reason to think that Paul knew other parables from the same context in Matthew's Gospel, for example the parable of the faithful and unfaithful stewards. A steward was the manager of a rich man's affairs, and Paul more than once speaks of his own ministry in terms of being a steward. For example in his first letter to the Corinthians he comments "it is required of stewards that they be found faithful" (4:2) – just as Jesus had taught.

Paul appears to have known much of the teaching in Matthew chapters 24 and 25 (which has parallels in Luke's Gospel), including the description of the Lord's return, the parable of the thief, and the parable of the girls at the wedding.

Conclusions

The past three chapters have explored some of the most important evidence for Paul knowing and drawing deeply on the stories and sayings of Jesus in the gospels. There are many more examples we could discuss. The cumulative effect is very weighty, supporting the view that Paul was soaked in the traditions of Jesus and that he taught them and passed them on to his converts and the church congregations that he founded.

The first impression that Paul used such traditions rather little – his silence, as it may appear – is not a sign of any lack of interest in Jesus nor of independence from Jesus. It is rather to be explained by the fact that he and his readers could take those stories for granted. In our New Testament today we have the gospels and the letters. Paul's readers did not have that the New Testament, obviously, but they had a tradition that was like the gospels and had been passed on and received, and this is the background to the letters and teaching of Paul.

CHAPTER 7

Was Paul the Inventor of Christian Doctrines?

It is Paul's supposed silence about Jesus' life and ministry which lends some plausibility to the view that he was not very interested in the real Jesus. It is only a short step from that conclusion to the argument that Paul was a creative thinker who transformed the teaching of the good prophet Jesus into a mystery religion deriving largely from his imagination. However, the last three chapters have shown that there is plenty of evidence pointing to Paul's knowledge of the stories and sayings of Jesus, and showing that he taught them to his converts as something of foundational importance.

It might be possible to admit this, but still to claim that Paul was very creative, interpreting the teaching of Jesus to suit himself and introducing major theological innovations into the Christian church, for example the idea of Jesus saving sinful humankind through his sacrificial death and the idea of Jesus as God in human form. These two ideas – of *atonement* (Jesus' death achieving forgiveness and salvation for the human race) and *incarnation* (God becoming a man) – would become some of the most important doctrines for Christians throughout history. Was Paul responsible for them?

Richard Dawkins sees things this way in *The God Delusion* and makes the point with typical forcefulness: "But now the sado-masochism. God incarnated himself as a man, Jesus, in order that he should be tortured and executed in *atonement* for the hereditary sin of Adam. Ever since Paul expounded this repellent doctrine, Jesus has been worshipped as the *redeemer* of all our sins."[1]

Did Paul invent the idea of the atonement?

To address this question it is necessary to retrace some of the steps of previous chapters. Paul certainly learned things about God and sin through his conversion experience: he discovered himself to be the worst of sinners, and he could well have concluded that Jesus' crucifixion happened to atone for such sins. The Old Testament, which he as a keen Pharisee knew so well, had at its very heart the idea of blood sacrifices (of animals) taking away sin. Paul could have concluded that the crucifixion was the final atoning sacrifice. Was he the first to make that imaginative theological leap?

That is not likely.

The crucifixion of Jesus is a fact

In the first place, it is important to emphasize that Paul did not invent the idea of Jesus being crucified. The crucifixion is attested by non-Christian sources, and the accounts in the gospels fit with what we know about the Palestine of Jesus' day: there were Romans such as Pilate, local warlords such as Herod, and Jewish leaders such as Caiaphas all involved in deadly political games. And the idea of their "Lord" and messiah being crucified and so saving the world would hardly have been invented by the early Christians since it would have seemed bizarre! Paul himself says this in the first chapter of 1 Corinthians.[2]

But if Paul did not invent the crucifixion, did he come up with the idea that it was a sacrifice for human sins? Was this his innovation? Three points tell against that view:

1. Jesus was a notorious friend of sinners
First, there is plenty of evidence that Jesus himself was famous for his own interest in "sinners". It is one of the least disputable things about him. Jesus was criticized by the other religious leaders of his day for fraternizing with irreligious and immoral people, but he defended himself by explaining his role as being that of a doctor to the spiritually sick.[3]

2. A logical Christian explanation of the death of Jesus received by Paul
There is every probability that the Christians before Paul will have seen Jesus' death as a sacrifice for sins. How else would people from a Jewish background have explained it theologically? Paul clearly implies this in 1 Corinthians 15, when he identifies "he died for our sins" as part of the tradition that he learned and passed on to the Corinthians.[4]

3. The evidence of the Last Supper: Jesus on his own death
In first Corinthians Paul refers to the events of the Last Supper and describes how Jesus took some of the bread that was served at the meal and said "This is my body which

is for you", and how later he took a cup of wine, and said "This cup is the new covenant in my blood." Jesus went on: "As often as you eat this bread and drink the cup, you proclaim the Lord's death until he comes."

Jesus' language about body and blood at the Last Supper is paralleled in the Gospels of Matthew, Mark, and Luke – with some variations in wording. The language may sound rather esoteric, and the ritual certainly became very esoteric in some periods of Christian history, with magical and other ideas attached to it. But Paul has a rather simple explanation when he says that through it "you proclaim the Lord's death until he comes". He sees the Lord's Supper as given by Jesus to his followers as a way of remembering and celebrating his death, his crucifixion.

The language used about the bread and the cup shows that Jesus' death is seen as a sacrifice "for you"; the reference to "the new covenant in my blood" echoes Old Testament passages where God makes an agreement or covenant with God's people.[5] There God is the saviour of the people; the blood refers to a sacrifice that was offered in that connection. So now Jesus' death is seen as a sacrifice, bringing forgiveness and a new relationship between God and the people.

What is notable about this is that Paul traces these words and ideas back to the ministry of Jesus. He speaks of the whole story as something that he "received", and he says that the words about the body and blood were Jesus' own words. So the idea of Jesus' death being a sacrifice that saves goes back to Jesus himself.

This is Paul's evidence, and his evidence is plausible. As has been shown, the supper makes sense in the context of the Passover festival, of Jesus' journey to Jerusalem, and of his parabolic teaching. Jesus' disciples appear from the gospel accounts to have found it almost impossible to understand why Jesus would allow himself to be crucified; it was so contrary to their idea of what a messiah should do and be like. Through his acted parable Jesus vividly showed them that his death was "for you", a sacrifice to be received, establishing a new covenant. And it was all in the context of Passover, the great celebration of God's salvation and liberation of his people.

The evidence is that Jesus himself saw his death as a new Passover sacrifice, bringing spiritual liberation. It is striking that when Paul does refer to Jesus as "our Passover lamb" he does so almost incidentally in the course of making a different point; it is not an idea that he is emphasizing, but one with which he knows his followers will already be familiar. It is part of what Paul received.

Did Paul invent the Christian doctrine of incarnation – the idea of Jesus as God?

But was Jesus' divinity part of what Paul received? Or was this perhaps Paul's contribution to Christianity? Did he turn Jesus the Jewish prophet into a Greek divinity?

Paul does not emphasize Jesus' divinity
A first but important point is that Paul does not emphasize Jesus' divinity much in his letters. He speaks of Jesus as the Christ or messiah and as "the Lord". But, unlike later Christians, he only rarely speaks of Jesus as God's Son, and

almost never calls Jesus God directly. This has sometimes worried Christians who would like him to be more clearly orthodox!

In fact there is no real doubt that Paul does believe in the divinity of Jesus. It is very striking how in the letters he greets people in the name of God *and* of Jesus, bracketing them together, for example, "Grace and peace to you from God our Father and the Lord Jesus Christ".[6] He can echo the ancient Jewish creed in which God is one Lord, and include Jesus within that creed: "there is one God the Father... and one Lord Jesus Christ." He is clear in upholding Jewish monotheism, and yet somehow Jesus is included as divine with the Father.[7]

But although Paul does see Jesus as divine Son of God in these and many other passages, he does not labour the point. There is no evidence that it is a controversial point of view, which he needs or wants to argue for and which he is trying to propagate.

The one letter of Paul that may appear to contradict this assertion is the one to the Christians of Colosse, in central Turkey, because in this letter Paul does emphasize Jesus' divinity and his supremacy over creation – he is the "image of the invisible God, the firstborn..." Paul also emphasizes the importance of the crucifixion of Jesus: "For God was pleased to have all his fullness dwell in him, and through him to reconcile to himself all things, whether things on earth or things in heaven, by making peace through his blood, shed on the cross."[8] Here it does look as though Paul is opposing a human view of Jesus and insisting on his divine view.

But the Colossian Christians had probably come to

faith as a result of Paul's mission in the big city of the area, namely Ephesus. And their view was not a very early Christian view of Jesus as a human prophet, but was more likely a deviation from Paul's teaching. They had a tendency toward religious speculation and probably saw Jesus as some sort of spirit, but not as the divine Saviour. Paul therefore does seem more argumentative here.

Colossians is usually seen as one of the later extant letters of Paul; some people even think that it was written by someone else after Paul's time, in his name. This is improbable, but in any case the fact remains that the demonstrably early letters of Paul do not show us someone fighting for Jesus' divinity against other established Christians. Quite to the contrary; the evidence is that Paul inherited his views of Jesus from those who preceded him.

"Abba" again

A small but important piece of evidence in this regard is the point noted earlier about Paul's use of the Aramaic word "Abba" to refer to God in his letters to the Galatians and Romans. The case for this word going back to Jesus himself is very strong: it was something striking and very memorable about Jesus that he (unlike other religious leaders) addressed God in this way.

The importance of this for the discussion of Jesus' divinity is that it shows that the idea of Jesus as Son of God was not invented by Paul, or indeed by any other early Christian. It had its roots in Jesus' own intimate experience of God. Jesus "invented" this idea, not his followers – except that invention is hardly the word to use of someone who so evidently did have a special relationship with God.

Jesus' use of the word "Abba" does not necessarily prove that he understood himself to be divine in the way that Christians later came to present him as the second person in a divine Trinity. Indeed Jesus may well have taught his disciples to pray to God as "Abba" too: some people think that the Lord's Prayer, the model prayer that Jesus taught his disciples, began in Aramaic with "Abba". And Paul, as we have seen, speaks of Christians calling God "Abba". But Paul is clear that this Christian experience of God as father comes from Jesus and through his Spirit: it is "the Spirit of his Son" that brings Christians into a wonderful relationship of intimacy with God as "Abba" alongside Jesus – as his brothers and sisters.

So it would be wrong to claim that the use of the word in itself prove that the user is divine. But what is quite clear is that this usage goes back to Jesus and began in his own distinctive experience of God. So when Paul thinks of Jesus as God's Son this is not his idea at all, but one of the essential ingredients of Christianity that has its roots firmly in the ministry and teaching of Jesus.

The resurrection again

And then there is the resurrection of Jesus. For Paul the resurrection was vital to his faith as a whole. At the end of his first letter to the Corinthians there is a long discussion of the Christian hope for resurrection after death; he speaks of Jesus' resurrection as key evidence not just for the idea of resurrection in general, but for the whole of the Christian faith. He says: "if Christ has not been raised, our preaching is useless and so is your faith".[9]

Specifically, Paul links the resurrection of Jesus to his

divinity. In his famous letter to the Christians in Rome Paul begins by referring to the "gospel of God" – the Christian good news. He speaks of it in thoroughly Jewish terms, talking about the "Holy Scriptures" of the Old Testament and about Jesus as descended from the Jewish king David. And then he speaks of Jesus as "marked out as Son of God in power... by resurrection of the dead".[10] He does not mean that Jesus became Son of God through the resurrection, but he does mean that the resurrection of Jesus declared to all who would hear that Jesus was Son of God, as well as the Jewish messiah and Lord of everything.

Then in his letter to the Christians in Philippi Paul speaks of Jesus' amazing humility in becoming human and dying by crucifixion, and goes on to say: "Therefore God exalted him to the highest place and gave him the name that is above every name, that at the name of Jesus every knee should bow, in heaven and on earth and under the earth, and every tongue confess that Jesus Christ is Lord, to the glory of God the Father."[11] The language here about knees bowing comes from the Old Testament; and the "name that is above every name" is the name of God the Lord. Paul unambiguously connects Jesus' resurrection with divinity.

It is important to say that resurrection and divinity do not necessarily always go together – in ancient or modern religious thinking. The gospels have several accounts of Jesus as healer raising people from the dead, and those raised are not therefore seen as divine – just very unusual! A modern Jewish scholar has written a book arguing that Jesus was raised from the dead, but he sees Jesus simply as a prophet of God, not as divine. Even miraculous ascension to heaven does not prove divinity: Elijah in the

Old Testament is portrayed as ascending to heaven in a chariot, but he was only a prophet. And the Muslim view is that Jesus ascended to heaven, but likewise that he is only an important prophet.

However, the resurrection of Jesus was without question a massively significant event; after all crucified religious leaders do not normally come back to life! The evidence suggests that the first Christians, such as Paul, saw Jesus' resurrection as something quite sensational; and that it was decisive in establishing their faith in him as divine.

This was not just because Jesus was alive again, but, first, because of the nature of the resurrection appearances as experienced and reported by the disciples: the gospels portray the risen Jesus as a supernatural figure who came to them, appearing and disappearing. Paul's experience on the Damascus road was equally, if not more, supernatural.

Secondly, the importance of the resurrection had to do with the early Christians' experience of Jesus before his death, since he had extraordinary power as a healer which astonished those around him. He acted with great authority, claiming to be bringing God's "kingdom" to earth. He claimed to forgive people their sins – a divine prerogative. He claimed authority over the Sabbath – the God-appointed day of rest, and over the temple, God's house. And, as we have seen, he spoke of God as his father, his Abba, in a revolutionary way.

The evidence for Jesus being like this comes from the gospels, of course, but it is credible evidence. It helps explain why Jesus ended up crucified, because of the offence he caused some of the religious leaders. His disciples maintained their faith in this mysterious man, until his sad end which promised to shatter their faith. But then there was Easter, the day when they experienced him as alive again.

In those circumstances their conclusion was bound to be that Jesus had been vindicated by God, along with his controversial behaviour and claims. The crucifixion had seemed just the opposite: it seemed to disprove everything. But now the conclusion was that this Jesus was "both Lord and Christ", in the words attributed to Peter in the first Christian sermon.[12] These words are not a direct or explicit affirmation of divinity, but they are well on the way to that view of Jesus. The resurrected Jesus was not the human or political messiah they had perhaps been anticipating, but "Lord" in a much stronger sense.

A small but significant piece of evidence confirming that Jesus was seen in this way before the time of Paul is Paul's use of the Aramaic word *Maranatha*, "our Lord come", at the very end of his first letter to the Corinthians. As we have seen, this probably reflects the early Christians' eager anticipation of Jesus' return, and it was an invocation or prayer urging Jesus to come back. The fact that Paul uses the Aramaic expression in his letter to the Greek-speaking Corinthians suggests that it was an expression used in the worship of the very first Christians in Jerusalem, which then got exported into that of Christians elsewhere, such as Corinth. If this is right, then it shows that they believed strongly in Jesus as Lord. And if *Maranatha* is a prayer, as it probably is, then this is significant since the Jews were extremely clear that prayer can only be directed to God, not to any lesser being. The evidence, then, is that the pre-Pauline church recognized Jesus not just as a human lord, but as divine. This is not to say that they understood the Christian doctrine of the Trinity as it later came to be explained and defined, but they did see Jesus as more than just human, much more.

To conclude this discussion of the resurrection:

1. Paul was not the inventor of the idea of Jesus' resurrection. It was something that the first Christians believed in and which motivated them. Paul at first denied it when he was a persecutor of the church, but then came to accept it, after his Damascus Road experience.[13]

2. In theory it might be possible to argue that the early Christians believed in a purely human Jesus whom God raised from the dead and that it was Paul who made the jump from a belief in Jesus' resurrection to the idea of him as a divine being. But the evidence is strongly against this. The Christians before Paul were already worshipping Jesus as Lord and messiah. Their movement was growing rapidly because they were persuading people that Jesus was more than a prophet; Paul initially opposed the movement for the same reason. It is possible to argue that he developed and filled out their ideas, but he certainly cannot be credited with turning a human Jesus into a divine Christ.

The idea of Jesus as divine Son of God had its roots in Jesus' ministry, not least in his own consciousness of his divine authority and sonship. It was decisively confirmed to his followers through the resurrection. Paul at first resisted the idea, but then accepted it, thanks to his Damascus road experience. That experience was very important to him, but there is no good evidence that Paul was the originator of the idea of the divine Jesus.

Greek ideas and Jewish ideas

Paul's ideas about the atoning death of Jesus and Jesus as divine go back before Paul himself; they have their roots in the Aramaic-speaking church and indeed in Jesus' own ministry in Palestine. But it has been suggested that these ideas had their origins in Greek religious thought, and that it was Paul who brought them into Christianity. The suggestion is that the first Christians were Jews who saw Jesus simply as a human prophet and perhaps as their messiah, and that Paul introduced the ideas that Jesus was divine and that his death was sacrificial under the influence of Greek and Roman religion.

Not Greek

This view is wholly implausible. Yes, the Greek mystery religions may have ideas about being united with dying and rising gods (though these were not as widespread as one might deduce from some modern writers). And, yes, traditional Greek and Roman religion was full of mythological stories of gods coming down to earth. But it is entirely improbable that this has anything to do with Paul's understanding of Jesus. He came out of a strongly Jewish background, and Jews were very hostile to such pagan religion. There is no reason why his vision of Jesus on the Damascus road would have changed his mind on this matter. The evidence of Paul's letters is that it did not. For example, in the first chapter of his letter to the Romans he speaks very negatively (and very Jewishly) of idolatry.

But could he then have been influenced by the imperial religion which hailed the Roman emperor as Lord and used divine language about him? It may well be that Paul is responding to such religion at various points in his letters. But, again, the divinization of the emperor was deeply offensive to Jews and, although Paul would certainly have wanted to see Jesus as a greater Lord than Caesar, it is completely unlikely that this was the source of his thinking about Jesus' divinity.

But Jewish

After his conversion Paul did not abandon his Jewish monotheistic convictions. His thinking continued to be deeply rooted in the Old Testament Scriptures, with their uncompromising rejection of pagan gods and idols. In fact it is much more likely that his understanding of Jesus as divine Son of God reflects his Jewish background than Greco-Roman religion. This may seem a surprising suggestion, given the uncompromising monotheism of most Jews. Each day faithful Jews would recite the *Shema*, affirming: "Hear, O Israel: the Lord our God, the Lord is one"[14] However, within Jewish monotheistic thinking there were various ideas that almost certainly influenced the first Christians in their understanding of Jesus as Son of God. Two are especially important:

- First, the Old Testament can speak of Israel's king as God's son. "You are my Son", says Psalm 2; and in the second book of Samuel God speaks to David about his son Solomon and says "I will be his father and he will be my son."[15] The Jews came to look forward to the coming of a future messiah, a king in the line of David, and he too could be spoken of as God's son. We find that sort of language in some of the famous Dead Sea Scrolls, which go back to about the time of Jesus.

When the Old Testament speaks of the king as God's son, the picture is of God adopting the king as his son and deputy, and it is not a declaration of divinity in the way that we might understand it; nor was it seen as compromising monotheism in any way. But it was a concept that Christians could and would naturally apply to their messiah, Jesus, without compromising their monotheism. Their convictions about Jesus' resurrection would have made the identification of Jesus as Son of God all the more obvious, but could and would also have suggested a greater sonship than that of Solomon and other sons of David.

A second idea in Judaism that helped prepare the way for seeing Jesus as divine concerned the nature of God's working. Judaism was emphatically, almost militantly, monotheistic; and yet the one God was seen to be a wonderful God with many attributes and with many angelic and human servants.

One of God's attributes was *wisdom*, and in the Old Testament as well as in later Jewish writings God's wisdom came to be pictured as a person working with God, helping in the divine work of creation and salvation. The Old Testament book of Proverbs uses this picture in chapter 8, and it is important in the later Jewish book of Wisdom, which was written not all that long before the New Testament. This picture was not seen as compromising monotheism, but was one attractive way of describing the wonderful workings of the one true God in the world.

This appears to be another concept that the Christians took from Judaism and began to use to "explain" Jesus. In various striking passages in the New Testament, such as the famous opening of John's Gospel (the passage that starts: "In the beginning was the Word…"[16]), there are clear echoes of Jewish wisdom teaching, all now applied to Jesus. It is the probable background to Paul's teaching about Jesus' supremacy in his letter to the Colossians; and in his first letter to the Corinthians he directly speaks of Jesus as "the wisdom of God".[17]

A remarkable mutation

To say that such Jewish ideas contributed to early Christian thinking about Jesus is not to say that Christian convictions about Jesus' divinity are easily explained in terms of this background. Jews did not conventionally describe great teachers or leaders as divine or as God's wisdom, and to describe someone from very recent history – who, incidentally, had been crucified by the Romans – as divine was astonishing. It is a very remarkable "mutation" of ideas, to use a word from the notable Edinburgh scholar Larry Hurtado.[18] The mutation reflects the extraordinary impact of Jesus – things like his use of "Abba" and, especially, his resurrection.

The importance of this for the present discussion of Paul is that it completely undermines any idea of Paul importing

ideas of Jesus' divinity and Jesus' death into Christianity
from Greco-Roman religion. Of course, it would be
possible to shift the argument and to say that it was he who
developed such Christian thinking out of Jewish thought.
But there are plenty of reasons for thinking that Paul was
not the source of the ideas in question.

CHAPTER 8

Did Paul and Jesus Really Agree?

The case for Paul being the mind behind Christianity as we know it is very unpersuasive. Paul seems to have used the teachings and the story of Jesus a great deal; and the key Christian ideas about Jesus' divinity and about his death being a sacrifice for sin were not Paul's imaginings, but go back to the pre-Pauline church and even into the ministry of Jesus.

But before concluding that the case is proved, it is necessary to address three questions that might point in a different direction:

First: despite everything, are there not huge differences between Paul and Jesus? Was Paul really in accord with Jesus?

Second: what about the argument that the gospels all come from Paul's part of the church? If that were the case, Paul's agreement with the Jesus of the gospels would not prove anything.

Third: is it possible to claim that Paul was not an innovator, given the evidence in the New Testament that he was such a controversial figure in the first Christian church?

These questions will be addressed in the next three chapters, before a final conclusion is reached.

The differences between Paul and the Jesus of the gospels

Is it really the case that Paul was a faithful follower of Jesus in his teaching? Are Paul's very theological letters not a world away from Jesus' justly famous teaching, as we find it in the gospels? People who hear Paul's letters read in church – or who try to read the letters themselves – often feel that they are in a different world from that of Jesus. Apart from anything else Paul is often difficult to follow, whereas the stories and sayings of Jesus are typically interesting and accessible.

And it is not just the form and accessibility that are different, but the contents, in the way that Jesus' and Paul's teachings are often understood. Jesus is seen as a caring teacher and healer. He mixed with ordinary people, mainly in rural Galilee, especially people in need and on the margins of society, including women and children. He taught about God's fatherly love for all, for example through his parable of the Prodigal Son – the classic story of a rebel son who wastes his family inheritance but who is forgiven and welcomed back by his father. Jesus condemned hypocritical religion, and especially hypocritical religious leaders. He gave wonderful ethical teaching, and he taught that men and women should love each other and even that they should love their enemies. His parable of the Good Samaritan is famous, and is particularly powerful when we recognize the historic hostility that existed between Jews and Samaritans.

If this is how Jesus is seen, Paul is often regarded as a dogmatic and narrow-minded theologian and missionary. He taught about the "wrath of God" against human sin, notably sexual sin (including homosexuality). He saw the death of Jesus as a sacrifice placating the wrath of the angry God, and wrote about people being justified through faith in Jesus and through baptism. He thought in legal terms about God the judge and about being guilty or not guilty. He had mystical ideas about dying and rising with Jesus and experiencing the Holy Spirit. He was quite authoritarian in his ethical teaching – so it is said – putting down women, having little time for sex, marriage, or the physical body, and not speaking out against slavery and injustice. He had great ideas about his own importance as a missionary to the Gentile world, whereas Jesus worked among his own Jewish people.

In other words, Jesus and Paul were saying very different things. This is confirmed, supposedly, by the simple observation that Jesus' main theme was "the kingdom of God" and his favourite way of speaking of himself was as "Son of Man" – phrases that will be explained a little later. Paul, on the other hand, refers to the kingdom of God very little and never to Jesus as Son of Man. So perhaps there is something to be said after all for the view that Paul founded a new religion, which we know as Christianity, and which was very different from the religion of Jesus.

But is this reading of things persuasive? Despite its popularity, the facts do not bear it out. The descriptions given of Jesus and Paul represent a caricature of Jesus to some extent, and of Paul to a great extent. In order to show this, it is necessary to look at some key features of Jesus' teaching as described in the gospels and to compare it with Paul's.

Such a broad-brush comparison is in some ways more speculative than the arguments of this book so far, since the topics are so huge and there are different opinions among scholars. What follows in this chapter is one reasonable account: it does not claim to be definitive, but it is a response to those who see a gulf between Jesus as he appears in the gospels and Paul.

Yes, the teaching of Jesus differs from that of Paul

Before embarking on a comparison of the teachings of Jesus and Paul, it is worth saying very clearly that there is no problem with recognizing that there will have been, and actually were, real differences between them. They were different people in different contexts doing different things.

To be more specific:

1. Jesus and Paul came from different backgrounds

Jesus was born and brought up and ministered in Palestine, mainly in villages and small towns in semi-rural Galilee, and he had no formal "higher education", as it might be called it today. Paul was born in a Greco-Roman city outside Palestine, came from a family with some status, and was trained in a top rabbinic school in Jerusalem. So it is not surprising if he sometimes seems more difficult to understand than Jesus; he uses rabbinic styles of argument that are quite foreign to many people today. Not that Jesus' teaching is always simple to understand; it is often profound, challenging, and sometimes puzzling. The gospels describe his critics as being astonished at his understanding, given his lack of academic training; he spoke with an "authority" that put the official theologians – the scribes – in the shade.

2. Jesus and Paul were addressing different audiences using different languages

Jesus' teaching was addressed primarily to ordinary Aramaic-speaking Jewish people in Galilee, Paul in his letters was primarily addressing Greek-speaking people from cities in the non-Jewish Mediterranean world. Teaching that immediately made sense in Jesus' context, for example about Samaritans or Pharisees, would be literally foreign to many of Paul's readers. This is very likely to be the reason that Paul does not emphasize the "kingdom of God" in the way that Jesus does. Even the switch from one language to another, from Jesus' Aramaic to Paul's Greek, will sometimes mean putting things differently, as anyone who tries to translate from French or Chinese into English or vice versa will know.

3. Jesus and Paul were teaching at different times

Although Paul was teaching and ministering only a few years after Jesus, he was teaching after Jesus' death and resurrection. He was also teaching after the coming of the Holy Spirit on the followers of Jesus at Pentecost. Jesus had been known as a charismatic person with great spiritual power (seen most obviously in his healings); after his death and resurrection his followers began to share this ministry, and it was a key feature of the Christian community. Paul was also writing, of course, after his own conversion experience and in the context of his own missionary work. This context was quite different from that of Jesus prior to his crucifixion. Jesus was involved in public preaching and in teaching his own disciples; his death lay in the future. Paul was writing after the pivotal events of Jesus' death and resurrection; and his letters are dominated on the one hand by those hugely important events, and on the other by things going on in the spiritually dynamic communities to which he was writing.

4. Letters are different from preaching the gospel
Paul's letters were largely troubleshooting documents, responding to issues that had arisen in the churches to which he wrote. This is one of the major reasons why they sometimes seem difficult; they are a little like listening to one end of a telephone conversation when you do not know what is being said at the other end. It is likely that Paul's preaching was much more accessible than his letters: he clearly told people the story of Jesus and passed on Jesus' teaching to them, including vivid parables such as that of the thief and that of the wise and foolish girls. Paul's own teaching was probably not all like his letters!

But their basic ideas are the same

Despite their real differences, however, the main emphases of Jesus (as we meet him the gospels) and Paul (as we know him through his letters) are very much the same.

1. The kingdom of God

In Jesus' teaching

The most important theme of Jesus' teaching in the gospels is the kingdom of God. "The kingdom of God has come near", proclaims Jesus in Matthew, Mark, and Luke.[1]

The background to this message is almost certainly to be found in Jesus' first-century Palestinian context. The country had been under the rule of the Romans since 63 BC and the Jews hoped for liberation from the foreign, pagan super-power. They looked back to prophecies in the Old Testament which spoke of God intervening to liberate the people. The Old Testament prophets had been thinking about the liberation from exile in Babylon (modern Iraq), but in Jesus' time people were looking for the prophecies to be fulfilled in terms of liberation from the Roman empire. One such prophecy speaks of "those who bring good news, who proclaim peace, who bring good tidings, who proclaim salvation, who say to Zion, "Your God reigns!"[2] It sometimes – often – seemed to the Jews that the God they worshipped was not reigning; it was as though pagan gods were reigning. But the prophet looks forward to God saving the people and ruling them.

How was this going to happen? One major element of hope in the Old Testament was that God would send a king who would save the people. This king would come from the family of the great Old Testament king David (who lived about 1000 BC). Kings were anointed, and the Hebrew word for someone anointed was "messiah". So the hope was for a *messiah*. This hope was very much alive in Jesus' time, though it took various forms, with some people looking for a messiah who would lead them in attacking their Roman overlords while others had a more spiritualized idea. Some hoped not just for one messiah, but for two: one a king and one a priest.

When Jesus announced that "the kingdom of God has come near", it was an exciting message for his hearers, suggesting that the longed-for liberation had come. Some undoubtedly hoped that this meant political liberation and that Jesus himself would be the sort of nationalist messiah who would lead the Jews against the Romans. Jesus himself, however, saw the kingdom and his ministry in more spiritual and social terms: he was a remarkable healer and exorcist, with spiritual power – "full of the Holy Spirit" as the New Testament puts it. And he described himself overcoming the strong man Satan, not the strong man Caesar.[3] The coming of the "kingdom" or "rule" of God meant overcoming evil in the world, and restoring God's reign in that way. Jesus appears to have seen his ministry as fulfilling God's promises and inaugurating a new world of liberation – a new world of healing, reconciliation, and forgiveness.

Jesus did not see the kingdom as coming all at once: he compared it to the sowing of seed; the harvest lies in the future. And so there is a sense of excitement in Jesus' teaching as to what was beginning with his ministry, but he also taught his disciples to pray "Your kingdom come", and he spoke in his parables about the "master" going away for a time and leaving his servants to get on with his work.[4]

In Paul's teaching

At first sight Paul looks quite at odds with Jesus on this very fundamental matter. He refers to "the kingdom of God" rather seldom in his letters, and this could seem to confirm that he is not even trying to pass on the teachings of Jesus. However, at least three points are worth making:

• It is true that Paul does not often use the phrase "kingdom of God". But he very clearly does see Jesus as bringing the new day of deliverance promised by God in the Old Testament and anticipated by the Jewish faithful. So in the very first verses of his letter to the Romans he refers to the "good news [gospel] of God, which he promised beforehand through his prophets in the Holy Scriptures, concerning his Son…".[5] Later in the chapter he refers to "a righteousness from God" being revealed, as promised in the Old Testament and describes God bringing the promised day when things will be put right.[6] This is very close to what Jesus was saying in announcing the coming of the kingdom of God.

• When Paul does refer to "the kingdom of God" it is in a way that suggests he knows and has passed on the teaching of Jesus.

  Three examples make the point: in his first letter to the Corinthians Paul says "Do you not know that the unrighteous will not inherit the kingdom of God?"[7] This sounds very like what we find in the gospel accounts of Jesus' teaching, for example in the Sermon on the Mount where Jesus speaks of righteousness as essential for entering the kingdom of God. It is significant that Paul says to the Corinthians "Do you not know…?" He presupposes that they have heard this teaching before. It is a reasonable inference that Paul had passed on to them Jesus' teaching about the kingdom of God.

At another point in the same letter Paul says "For the kingdom of God does not consist in talk but in power";[8] and in his letter to the Romans he says "The kingdom of God is not food and drink, but righteousness and joy and peace in the Holy Spirit."[9] Paul's words recall the gospel accounts and their picture of Jesus, as a spiritually powerful leader bringing the kingdom and changing lives. And just as Jesus spoke of the kingdom as something present (through the work of the Holy Spirit) but also in the future, so Paul speaks of it as present in power, but also something to be inherited in the future.

- It seems very likely that "kingdom of God" was one of those phrases that worked well in the Jewish context of Jesus, but less well out among the Gentiles of the Roman world. The language of "king" and "kingdom" may have been rather sensitive in the Roman world, since it could be used against Christians as evidence of their political subversiveness. Acts describes Paul having problems in the Greek city of Thessalonica, and the accusation against the Christians is "they are all acting against the decrees of Caesar, saying that there is another king, Jesus."[10] Paul may well have wanted to avoid dangerous and distracting misunderstandings of Jesus. So he preferred to put things differently, for example by referring to God's "righteousness being revealed".[11]

2. Sinners and outsiders

In Jesus' ministry

One of the things that seems most to have characterized Jesus and his ministry was his mixing with "sinners". Other Jewish leaders and groups in Jesus' day were zealous in their observances and zealous for religious purity. With the Gentile Romans ruling the country, bringing with them non-Jewish culture and values, it was important to groups such as the Pharisees to maintain their Jewish distinctiveness. Jesus was a different religious leader, being flexible about things such as the Sabbath, and notorious for associating with non-religious "sinners" (including prostitutes and tax-collectors; the latter were viewed as corrupt servants of the foreign imperialists). Jesus was sharply criticized for this fraternizing.

But in Jesus' vision the coming of the kingdom of God, and his role within it, represented healing, both physical and spiritual. He justified mixing with sinners by comparing himself to a doctor, whose place is among the sick, not among the healthy. His parables often make the same point, for example the story of the lost sheep which the shepherd goes out to find, and of the prodigal son whom the father welcomes back with open arms.[12] Jesus offered God's forgiveness to people, in a way that offended his opponents, who asked where his authority came from.

Jesus saw the coming of God's rule not only spiritually, but also as the overcoming of injustice, including economic injustice; and so he is more than once described as bringing "good news to the poor". Several of his parables are sharp critiques of the rich, such as the story of the rich man and Lazarus. Lazarus is a beggar who sits at the rich man's gate;

but after death the beggar ends up in heavenly bliss, the rich man in the agony of hell.[13]

For Jesus the kingdom of God also meant the overcoming of social alienation and prejudice. He healed lepers, who were shunned by society because of their illness, and made a Samaritan the hero of one of his parables, illustrating his understanding of loving one's neighbour. Jesus honoured and associated with women in a way that was remarkable for a Jewish religious leader of the time. When his disciple Mary sat at Jesus' feet and listened to his teaching, she not only annoyed her sister Martha by not helping with the cooking, but also disregarded the cultural norm: male disciples of rabbis would sit listening to their masters, but women were not included. Jesus, however, defended and commended Mary.[14]

For Paul

Paul is often seen as a social conservative while Jesus is seen as a radical. But this is far from the truth. Just as Jesus was criticized by religious Jews for mixing with sinners, Paul in turn became notorious, even among some of his fellow Christians, because of his welcoming attitude toward Gentiles. He did not require them to come under the "yoke" of the Jewish law and urged Jewish and Gentile Christians to "welcome one another... As Christ has welcomed you", consciously grounding his attitude in that of Jesus.[15]

One of the famous emphases in Paul's writings is "justification by faith": he insisted that people achieve right relationship with God (are "justified"), not by keeping the law, or through religiosity or even morality, but through trust in God and God's mercy ("faith"). This emphasis was anticipated in Jesus' teaching: as a healer Jesus invited people to have faith, and as a teacher he explained that the way for sinful human beings to put themselves right with God was that of the prodigal son. The boy admitted that he had made serious mistakes and threw himself on the mercy of his father. For Paul both Jews and Gentiles are in exactly the same situation, saved by God's grace received through faith.

Paul's radicalism did not just extend to Gentiles, but to people all over the social spectrum. He associated with poor people, earning his keep through tent-making and leather-working instead of accepting the patronage of the wealthy, as many teachers of religion and philosophy did. There is some reason to think that he was criticized for this; but it was important for him not to profit from the gospel but to make it "free of charge", and not to give the impression that it was for the powerful and wealthy. He was successful in bringing the gospel to ordinary people, at least to judge from his own remarks to the Corinthian Christians that not many of them were "wise according to worldly standards, not many were powerful, not many were of noble birth".[16]

Some wealthy people did respond to Paul's ministry such as Erastus, the city treasurer of Corinth:[17] archaeologists have found an inscription in Corinth referring to an Erastus and they think that he is quite likely to be the one whom Paul knew, and he was an important man. But most Christians were not powerful, intellectually, economically, or socially. Slavery was practised in Roman society, and it is clear that there was a significant number of slaves in Paul's churches.

This was important for Paul: in one of his justly famous sayings he says "In Christ there is no Jew or Greek, no slave or free, no male and female, for you are all one in Christ Jesus."[18] This was something revolutionary.

People have questioned whether Paul lived up to this revolutionary ideal, arguing that he did not challenge slavery, and that he treated women as second-class citizens in the church. It is true that Paul does not command masters to release their slaves forthwith, and he even sent one runaway slave, Onesimus, back to his master, Philemon. The shortest of Paul's letters in the New Testament is the one he wrote to Philemon about Onesimus, who had become a Christian through Paul's ministry. However, Paul speaks with huge warmth about Onesimus, and urges Philemon to receive him back, not as a runaway slave who could be punished or even executed, but as a beloved brother in the Lord. Elsewhere Paul urges slaves to serve well, but he goes on to tell masters to "do the same to them" – to treat them well, remembering that the masters too have a master, Jesus, to whom they must give account.[19]

As for women, Paul writes with affection and enthusiasm about women who have worked as his colleagues and who have ministered in various ways in the church, including as prophets.[20] He commends them and is grateful to them for their friendship and support. There is no trace of Paul being a misogynist who "expresses both fear and contempt for the female", as the atheist writer Christopher Hitchens claims.[21]

There are a few places where Paul seems to undermine women, which often worry modern readers.[22] Some scholars have seen these passages where Paul restricts the role of women in the worship of the church as so unlike

Paul elsewhere as to put in question their authenticity. It has been speculated that some of the letters ascribed to Paul in the New Testament or some passages in the letters come from a follower of Paul who was less enlightened than he was and who was interpreting Paul accordingly. That would leave us with the real Paul being more radical, though still not as radical as some would like!

The more probable explanation in my view has to do with the likely context of Paul's remarks. It is likely that women in churches founded by Paul were indeed strikingly liberated; after all he taught that in Christ there is no male or female! But some of them were causing offence by behaving in disruptive or culturally inappropriate ways in church worship, for example abandoning the modesty of the time by praying with their heads unveiled. It looks as though they were arguing that no male or female means that Christians are unisex or should be unisex in their spirituality; it may have been similar thinking that led some of the Corinthian Christians to argue that truly spiritual people should have no sex at all.

Paul, contrary to the impression that some people have, is wholly opposed to this kind of ascetic spirituality. He does think that there is value in singleness for those with that "gift", but he is emphatically opposed to the prohibition or denigration of sex and marriage. Paul believed in creation, and in the Old Testament creation story which spoke of God creating man and woman, and of God creating marriage and sex.[23] He believed in the goodness of the human body, unlike some of his Greek contemporaries.[24] He believed the Old Testament affirmation that God's created order was very good. He did see husbands as having a leadership role within marriage, but emphasized that the way for husbands to exercise it was by loving their wives sacrificially, as Christ loved the church.

There has been a huge amount of discussion of the texts in question, to which it is not possible to do justice here. It is safe to say that Paul was not a modern feminist; but it is unlikely that Jesus was either! However, Paul was radically affirmative of women, of children, of slaves, of Gentiles, of marriage, of creation, and of the physical body. His claim to be "an imitator of Christ" has credibility, though he was addressing issues that Jesus did not have to face.[25]

3. Radical living

For Jesus

Jesus' view of the kingdom was inclusive – astonishingly so in the eyes of his contemporaries. But he was not ethically permissive. He called his disciples to a radical commitment to God's rule; and he saw this rule as meaning a kind of love and a giving of oneself to others that were revolutionary. The parable of the Good Samaritan most famously illustrates it, as does the Sermon on the Mount, with its call to "love your enemies".[26]

Jesus' call for a radically different way of life is seen also in his teaching about sex and marriage. He not only endorsed the Old Testament commandment "You shall not commit adultery", but he warned against adultery in the heart. And when asked about divorce, he presented the story of Genesis, in which God made man and woman to be one, as God's model for marriage.[27] In his teaching about money, Jesus called his followers to a radical sharing of their wealth with others.[28] For Jesus the coming of

God's rule in people's lives meant new lives and new attitudes – living as children of God the Father in God's perfect way.[29]

Jesus did not expect his disciples to achieve such perfection at once: he told them to pray "forgive us our sins".[30] But still the way of perfection was the way of the kingdom and discipleship. The gospels portray Jesus as being challenged more than once by his disciples about the impossibility of what he asked; his reply was that "It is impossible with human beings, but it is possible with God."[31] This reflects his belief that the Holy Spirit of God was at work in the coming of the kingdom and that through this spiritual power his disciples could begin to be changed.

Jesus' inclusiveness was thus not laxness – in ethics or in any other way. The invitation and the offer of the love of God was inclusive and for all, but the person who accepted the invitation and offer was entering a new life. Jesus spoke of the "narrow way" that leads to life, contrasting it with the "broad way" that leads to destruction.[32] Jesus is sometimes portrayed as only bringing good news and no bad news, and that is indeed his primary emphasis. But he was extremely forthright about the divine judgment on religious leaders who are "hypocrites" – the Greek word means something like "play-actors". And he was similarly forthright with the rich who looked after their own interests and did not care for the poor, and with those who claimed to be his disciples but who ignored his teaching.[33] Jesus' parables are not just nice stories; many of them are very serious warnings about divine judgment.

For Paul

The combination in Jesus' teaching of an inclusive understanding of grace for sinners and of God's love for all people with a perfectionist ethic focused on love is found also in Paul. He was accused by his opponents of being antinomian – in favour of lawlessness – because he taught that Christians are "free" from the Jewish law; but he did not tolerate some of the Christians in Corinth, who said that "all things are permissible", and who thus justified going to prostitutes and even being involved in the worship of pagan idols.[34] Paul believed that Christians were free from the Old Testament law; but in becoming Christians and in committing themselves to Jesus in baptism they had come into a relationship with Jesus and the Holy Spirit. This completely ruled out immorality and idolatry, and involved a new way of living in love – like Jesus and for Jesus – which was more demanding, but also more powerful, than living under the old law.

Paul, like Jesus, could speak of his desire and ambition to see his converts being more and more loving, and living pure and blameless lives filled with "the fruits of righteousness which come through Jesus Christ".[35] This is the Sermon on the Mount all over again. Paul, like Jesus, knew that Christians would sin and need forgiveness, but he was not complacent about it. He believed, like Jesus, in future judgment, and that religiousness without right actions is useless.

This is clear from Paul's most famous teaching on love, in his first letter to the Corinthians, where he is discussing the Corinthians' experience of the Holy Spirit. Just as Jesus had been a charismatic leader with spiritual power, especially the power to heal, the churches founded by Paul were likewise charismatic communities. One spiritual manifestation among them was "speaking in tongues" – inspired speech in languages unknown to the speaker. Paul recognizes such speech as a genuine spiritual gift, but nevertheless writes: "if I speak in tongues... if I have the gift of prophecy... if I have a faith that can move mountains... if I give all I possess to the poor... but have not love, I gain nothing."[36] In other words, spirituality without a changed life is empty.

Paul is totally at one with Jesus on this matter, and previous chapters have shown how he quotes or alludes to Jesus' teaching on ethical matters such as divorce, on "the law" of love, and on judgment (in parables such as those of the thief and of the wise and foolish girls).

4. Who was Jesus?

Jesus' own view

Jesus announced God's kingdom, and clearly saw it as coming in and through his ministry. But how did he see himself fitting into that coming? His authoritative teaching, his controversial forgiveness of sins, and his evident consciousness of a close relationship with God as his father ("Abba") all point to him having a sense of divine authority.

Interestingly, however, Jesus speaks most frequently of himself as "the Son of Man", a somewhat enigmatic phrase. It is a Semitic expression meaning something like "the human being". But why does Jesus call himself "the human being"? Christians have often thought that the divine Jesus used it in order to emphasize his humanity: Jesus is the divine Son of God, and the human Son of Man. However, it is doubtful if this is what Jesus meant. After all, his contemporaries hardly needed persuading of his humanity; he was walking, talking, eating among them as a human being.

The way the writers of the New Testament seem to understand the phrase is as referring to the Old Testament book of Daniel, where there is a colourful vision of four enormously strong wild animals and then of "one like a son of man" – a human figure.[37] This vision seems to be a prophecy: the animals represent four of the super-powers of the ancient world, under whose often oppressive rule the Jews, God's people, lived. The human figure represents the people. And the vision is of God stripping away the power of the beasts and giving it to the human figure. It is thus a prophecy, like other Old Testament prophecies, about God saving God's people.

So why did Jesus use the expression "Son of Man" to refer to himself? This was not to emphasize his humanity as such, but rather to express his role as the one who is bringing God's salvation. Contrary to a common assumption, it was not a way of emphasizing Jesus' humble humanity as opposed to his divinity; indeed in Daniel the one like a son of man receives "kingdom" and dominion over the world. Jesus may well have used it because it was a mysterious but striking claim to authority.

It is not far from this observation to the conclusion that Jesus saw himself as the messiah of Jewish expectation. Interestingly he does not very often or explicitly call himself the messiah, or the son of David. Scholars have pondered as to why he seems reluctant to use this language and even for his followers to use it. One plausible explanation is that Jesus wished to distance himself from the popular, politicized concept of the messiah; "Son of Man" was a more ambiguous and a safer way to speak of himself.

But the gospels make it clear that Jesus did see himself as the hoped-for king. This comes out as clearly as anywhere in the story of his entry into Jerusalem before his crucifixion, which he arranged so that he would enter the city riding on a donkey. The Old Testament prophet Zechariah, writing several centuries before the time of Jesus, had spoken of God's king coming into Jerusalem on a donkey.[38] A king might be expected to come on a war-horse; but Zechariah portrayed him coming humbly in this way.

The gospels suggest that Jesus' opponents recognized the idea of Jesus as messiah; indeed the formal charge against Jesus, which led to his crucifixion by the Romans, was that he was claiming to be "the king of the Jews".[39] The Romans would not have been very interested if Jesus was just a religious leader without political aspirations. But if he was claiming to be "king of the Jews", that was treasonable and dangerous and would justify crucifixion.

In Paul's view

Paul's perspective on Jesus, who he was, and what he came to do is inevitably different from Jesus' own perspective. Paul is writing after the crucifixion, the resurrection, and his own conversion experience, and after the coming of the Holy Spirit at Pentecost. He writes as a devotee of Jesus; Jesus is his Lord, one whom he worships.

There is no ambiguity for Paul about Jesus being the messiah of Jewish expectation, and indeed he almost always speaks of Jesus as "Jesus *Christ*". Some scholars think that the meaning of the word "Christ" – it is the Greek equivalent of messiah – has retreated into the background, and that it is simply functioning as an alternative name, almost like a surname. That is certainly not always the case for Paul. But, even if it were true, this would just underline how fundamental it was for Paul.

Paul and Israel

For Paul Jesus was emphatically the Christ, the messiah of Jewish expectation. Paul saw his own personal calling as that of reaching out to the Gentiles, but this did not represent an abandonment of his Jewish convictions about God working through the people of Israel, and now through Jesus as the messiah of Israel. For Paul the Gentiles were being brought into the people of God, into the family of Abraham. He speaks of "the Jew first and then the Greek", just as Jesus had spoken in his ministry of "the lost sheep of the house of Israel" as his priority.[40]

There is an interesting contrast between Jesus and Paul here. Jesus seems to have been cautious in referring to himself as messiah, probably because of its potentially misleading connotations in the politically sensitive situation before his death. Paul needs no such caution, both because he is writing after the death and resurrection of Jesus, and because in the Greek world the Hebrew word "messiah" would not have been so sensitive.

Paul's other favourite way of referring to Jesus is as "Lord", *kyrios*. This was a term with a wide range of meanings:

• It was a respectful way of addressing a superior, like "sir".

- The master of a slave was his *kyrios*.

- A political leader, notably the Roman emperor, was *kyrios*, and it became a sensitive issue for Christians as to whether they would say "Caesar is Lord" or not.

- The word also came to be used of God, as it was by Jews in their worship: they used it as a substitute for the unspeakably sacred name, Yahweh.

For Paul the word expressed many things when it referred to Jesus. It could speak of his sense of being a grateful slave of Jesus as master. But it also undoubtedly came to have the sense of divinity for Paul, as we have already seen. Some scholars have regarded this term as something of Greek origin, imported into Christianity by Paul. Here at last there may be some evidence for Paul bringing Jesus' divinity into Christianity. However, as usual, this conclusion is precarious:

- *Mar*, the Aramaic word for "lord", was already a very important word in the Aramaic-speaking church before Paul, for example in the prayer *Maranatha*.

- Jesus told parables about himself in which a "master" (*kyrios*) has dealings with his servants. It seems likely that Paul knew these parables, such as that of the two stewards.

- The gospels portray Jesus in a rather rabbinic-sounding discussion of Psalm 110, in which he is identified with the "lord" referred to in the Psalm who is invited to sit at God's right hand.[41]

So thinking of Jesus as "Lord" does not seem to be an innovation on Paul's part, even if it was a term that had particular importance for him following the resurrection and following his own conversion.

Paul's failure to use "Son of Man" in referring to Jesus could seem puzzling. Why did Paul not adopt this usage? There are two quite simple answers to this question: first, Jesus probably used the phrase because of its ambiguity. His followers, however, after the resurrection, will probably have felt that "the human being" was not adequate for what they wanted to say, quite unambiguously, about Jesus. They wanted to affirm that he was *christos* and *kyrios*, while in no way questioning that he was a human being.

Secondly, "Son of Man" is a very Semitic phrase and not very Greek. So, except when reporting Jesus' own words, Paul and the other New Testament authors, writing in Greek, do not use the phrase.

Interestingly, Paul does identify Jesus as a second Adam.[42] In the Old Testament book of Genesis Adam is the original human being, the father of the human race with his wife Eve. He was also the one who, with Eve, initiated human rebellion against God and brought death into the world. It was remarkable to say of Jesus who had very recently been walking around in Palestine, that he was a second Adam – someone who had undone Adam's disastrous sin. Paul could have been influenced by Jesus' use of "Son of Man", with its associations of authority and kingship.

The previous chapter explored at some length Paul's view of Jesus' divinity, and saw how this was not Paul's invention or imagination, but something that he received from those who were Christians before him and that had roots in Jesus' own life and teaching. Nothing in this chapter relating to the person of Jesus alters that conclusion; Paul approaches the subject from a different angle, but he is faithful to Jesus and does not depart significantly from him.

5. The Lord's death

In Jesus' view

The final and very important thing to note about Jesus' understanding of himself and his mission, as described in the gospels, is that he strongly sensed that it was his vocation to die for the people. The gospels suggest that Jesus' followers found this a very upsetting and puzzling idea; they expected and wanted a conquering messiah.

At the Last Supper Jesus explained his death in terms of the Passover. Passover was about liberation and involved a sacrifice, and Jesus seems to have interpreted his death in those terms. Parts of the Old Testament may have contributed significantly to this understanding, notably Isaiah chapter 53 where the "servant of the Lord" is portrayed, again in the context of liberation. The servant takes the punishment for the people's sins on himself and dies for them. Jesus is seen in the gospels as such a servant, giving his life to bring God's kingdom and liberation from Satan's rule.

In Paul's view

Paul's emphatic belief in the importance of Jesus' death has already been discussed. His perspective is different from Jesus' own: he is writing after the event, not before it. He sees the death of Jesus as:

• an event in which God's righteous judgment on human sinfulness is expressed and addressed;

- an event in which God's love for sinners is extraordinarily expressed;

- at the very heart of God's purposes for the world, undoing the cosmic damage done by Adam's rebellion against God;

- something of deep personal relevance, so that in his letter to the Galatians he refers to Jesus as "the Son of God, who loved me and gave himself for me";[43]

- something that Christians come to share: when they enter the water of baptism they "die with" him spiritually, receiving the forgiveness of sins. They are then called to live a new life modelled on Jesus' suffering and self-giving.

Paul's view of the death of Jesus is rich and complex. He has a developed theology of the crucifixion which goes beyond what is found in the gospels. But it is entirely consonant with them. And chapter 5 demonstrates how his view of the death of Jesus is firmly rooted in the story and the teaching of Jesus: Paul knows about the Lord's Supper and its significance; he sees Jesus as a Passover sacrifice, and as a servant to others. He is a profound interpreter of Jesus, not an inventor.

Conclusion

So was Paul in agreement with Jesus? At first sight he may seem quite different from the Jesus of the gospels. But when we analyze what the gospels say and what Paul says, we find that the message is essentially the same. The gulf that some people see between them is imaginary.

If the gospels' portrayal of Jesus is anyway near historical, then the earlier conclusions are confirmed. Paul has not come up with a new message. He did not mechanically or woodenly reproduce Jesus' teaching, but intelligently and even creatively applied it in new contexts. But in all the essentials he remained faithful to Jesus, as a grateful servant and follower.

CHAPTER 9

Is Paul Behind the New Testament Gospels?

If it is true that the gospels and Paul are essentially in harmony, might that not simply confirm the view that Paul is really the person behind the New Testament? Does the New Testament not represent the triumph of Paul's version of Christianity over other versions? Are our gospels, in particular, the ones that conformed to Paul's view, with other gospels being suppressed?

Such a case can be argued. After all:

- Paul's letters dominate the New Testament, with other disciples of Jesus, such as Peter and John, getting very little space. Paul's letters take up about nine times as much space as Peter's and twelve times as much as John's!

- The longest narrative sections of the New Testament are Luke's Gospel and the book of Acts, both probably written by Paul's companion and admirer Luke. Over half of the book of Acts is about Paul and his journeys.

- Mark's Gospel is seen by most modern scholars as the earliest gospel to have been written; but the New Testament itself shows us that Mark – probably the same Mark – worked with Paul as a colleague.[1]

- If Mark's Gospel was used by the writers of Matthew's and Luke's Gospels, as most scholars believe, and perhaps also by the author of John's Gospel, then most of the New Testament and all of the accounts of Jesus' life – Matthew, Mark, Luke, and John – can be said to come directly or indirectly out of a Pauline tradition.

This evidence is significant, and there is no denying the importance of Paul. But it is quite another thing to say that Paul theologically hijacked early Christianity, and that his individual view of Jesus' divinity and death triumphed over rival views.

A number of things are worth saying here:

1. The gospels agree with Paul, but they do not appear to be promoting a particular view

A divine Jesus
Matthew, Mark, and Luke do all speak of Jesus in ways that suggest his divinity. So, in his version of the Christmas story, Matthew has the baby Jesus called "Emmanuel", "God with us".[2] This does not necessarily point to Jesus being divine – people are called Emmanuel in some parts of the Christian word today! But, as Matthew's Gospel unfolds, it is clear that Jesus is someone is one to be worshipped (like God), and the gospel ends with the disciples worshipping Jesus on a mountain and Jesus sending them out to baptize "in the name of the Father, the Son and the Holy Spirit".[3]

Mark's Gospel also portrays Jesus as acting with divine authority, forgiving sins (and so horrifying the religious authorities), walking on water, and referring to himself as "the Son".[4] Luke is similar.

Matthew, Mark, and Luke all see the death of Jesus as a sacrifice bringing the forgiveness of sins.

Not a laboured defence

But what is striking about the portrayal of Jesus' divinity in the gospels is how understated it is, so that some scholars even question whether the gospel writers really believe in it. Likewise, the writers give a lot of space to describing the death of Jesus, but they offer very little theological explanation of it – frustratingly little for modern readers who want to know what they thought. The fact is that, although they undoubtedly wanted to persuade people to believe in Jesus as Lord and Saviour, none of them seems to be going out of his way to argue a case about Jesus' divinity or his atoning death, as we might expect if this was a controversial topic on which they had a strong opinion.

2. The New Testament gospel writers did not get their ideas from Paul

The case for Matthew, Mark, and Luke promoting a particular view of Jesus' divinity and atonement is not strong, and neither is the case for them being heavily influenced by Paul.

Matthew

Far from following an obviously Pauline line, the author of Matthew's Gospel seems to be doing almost the opposite.

One of Paul's main emphases was his championing of Gentile Christianity: he argued that Gentile converts to Christianity should not be required to keep the Old Testament law. Matthew, on the other hand, is a thoroughly Jewish gospel in its style and contents, and the author emphasizes that Jesus did not "come to destroy the law and the prophets" – the Old Testament – but to "fulfil it".[5]

Some people have seen Matthew as deliberately opposing Paul, for example in the Sermon on the Mount where Jesus denounces those who "loosen" the demands of the Old Testament law.[6] Is this a veiled attack on Paul and his liberal views on what should be required of Gentile converts?

This is probably not so, but Matthew's Gospel does seem to have been written in a Jewish-Christian context and with that mindset. And Matthew may have wanted to correct some of the converts of Paul (for example some of those in Corinth) who were using his emphasis on freedom from the law as an excuse for their immorality.

Matthew, then, cannot plausibly be seen as a champion for Pauline Christianity. It may be worth adding that, if the early tradition that the gospel was written by the Matthew who was one of Jesus apostles is correct (or even if the apostle had some part to play in its composition), then it is unlikely to contain novel doctrines invented by Paul. Either way, the evidence does not place Matthew obviously in Paul's camp.

Mark

The earliest evidence suggests that this gospel was written
by the Mark who was at one time Paul's younger colleague
and companion. But it points to Mark writing his gospel on
the basis of Peter's preaching when Peter was in Rome.

At the beginning of the second century AD a man called
Papias said that: "Mark became Peter's interpreter and
wrote accurately all that he remembered...of the things
said or done by the Lord." Papias could have been wrong,
but his view has recently been forcefully restated by the
distinguished scholar Professor Richard Bauckham in his
book *Jesus and the Eyewitnesses*.[7] If Papias was right, then the
gospel is far from having been fixed by Paul in some way. It
represents an account coming from as close to Jesus as you
could get.

And even if Papias was wrong about the link between
Mark and Peter, the case for Mark's Gospel coming from
someone with good historical sources of information is
strong. One small piece of evidence for this is in Mark's
account of the death of Jesus. Not only is the description
plausible in all sorts of ways – historically attested figures
such as Pilate, Caiaphas, and others are key players in the
story – but Mark refers to a man from Cyrene in North
Africa carrying the cross of Jesus to the place of execution.
He names this person as "Simon, the father of Alexander
and Rufus".[8] The question this raises is: why mention this
man's sons Alexander and Rufus? The only reasonable
explanation is that Mark knew them and he expected some
of his readers to know them. So the writer of Mark's
Gospel perhaps knew Simon, an actual participant in the
story of Jesus' crucifixion and, if not Simon, then certainly

his children; we are thus within touching distance of the history of Jesus.

Some people have suggested that we get even nearer with Mark's curious reference to a young man who escaped naked when the soldiers arrested Jesus; could this be Mark himself? There is no way of knowing.

So it is likely that Mark did know Paul, but there is no plausibility in the idea that his gospel represents Paul's gospel in particular: it is more likely to represent Peter's. In any case it derives from someone with good sources of information and it was written at a very early date.

Luke

As for Luke, he is the most likely to be taking a Pauline line, since tradition and the evidence of the book of Acts both point to him being a companion of Paul.

However, four things at least should be noted:

- First, in the "prologue" to his gospel, where he sets out his aims in writing it, Luke expresses the intention of writing a reliable, accurate account.[9]

- In his second volume, the book of Acts, his historical accuracy is confirmed again and again. As was noted earlier, he gets historical details right: the journeys of Paul that he describes follow the route of ancient roads, and his references to places are confirmed by archaeological finds. He gets the titles of local officials in different cities right. Despite some scholars' views, the details in Acts fit remarkably well with details in Paul's letters.

- Luke's accuracy in the later parts of Acts can be explained by the "we" passages: he gets the details right, because he was there. These passages help us to map Luke's movements, and they show that he spent a long time in Palestine around AD 60, while Paul was in prison. He therefore had a lot of time to talk to local people about Jesus and to do the research to which he refers in his prologue so as to produce a reliable and accurate account.

• Luke's portrayal of Paul in the book of Acts is written by someone who admires Paul, but it is not a whitewash. He is very explicit about Paul's grim record as a persecutor of the church. He makes it clear that Peter was the first leader of the church, bringing into it the first Jews, the first Samaritans, and the first Gentiles. Interestingly Luke does not see Paul, as Paul does himself, as an apostle alongside the twelve.

So there is no reason for supposing that Luke was a lackey of Paul and idolized him. His claim to be writing a careful historical account on the basis of good eyewitness accounts has credibility.

Example of convergence between Acts and Paul's letters

Paul's first letter to the Thessalonians was written just after Paul left Athens and went to Corinth. His references in it to people being converted through his ministry and to "wrath" overtaking the Jews fit remarkably with the description of Paul's ministry in Acts 17 and of his arrival in Corinth in Acts 18, where he meets up with Aquila and Priscilla, who had recently experienced the wrath of the emperor against the Jews in Rome.

But what about John?

John's Gospel is rather different. It does have a very deliberate focus on the divinity of Jesus, and it seems likely that it was written in face of controversy over Jesus' identity and divinity.

Arguing with Jews and Christians

It looks as though John was arguing with Jews who, not surprisingly, opposed the Christian view of Jesus as messiah and Son of God, but probably also with some Christians who were having doubts about Jesus' identity. The first letter of John, which is clearly related to the gospel and is likely to have been written by the same person, refers to a split in a particular church congregation over the identity of Jesus: the author of the letter speaks of "antichrists" having gone out from "among us".[10] It is uncertain whether those who split were denying the divinity of Jesus or his humanity! Whatever the exact situation, John's Gospel emphasizes the divinity of Jesus, hence its famous opening words: "In the beginning was the Word and the Word was with God and the word was God." But it also emphasizes the fact that the word "became flesh", in other words Jesus' humanity.[11]

From John not Paul

John's evidence suggests that there was a split in the early church, with some people questioning Jesus' divinity, but it does not suggest that Paul was responsible for the view of Jesus as divine. John's Gospel cannot plausibly be assigned to a Pauline faction within the early church: it is a very distinctive account with distinctive language and emphases, and it does not sound very like Paul, despite some similar themes.

The gospel claims to be based on the testimony of an eyewitness of Jesus' ministry, someone it calls "the disciple whom Jesus loved".[12] The second-century tradition is that it was written by John, one of Jesus' disciples. According to the tradition it was the last of our gospels to be written, and that is also the opinion of most modern scholars, who date it to the last decade of the first century. It cannot be dated much later, given the very ancient fragment of the gospel mentioned earlier, which comes from around AD 125. If the gospel was indeed written towards the end of the first century, and directly or indirectly on the basis of the "loved disciple's" testimony, then it is completely irrelevant to the supposed (or imagined) controversy about the divinity of Jesus between the first followers of Jesus and Paul the innovator.

What John shows is that the question of Jesus' identity was not settled from the time of the resurrection onwards. It was questioned by Jews, inevitably, and it was debated among Christians, also inevitably. It would go on being debated among Christians for centuries, as the church discussed and hammered out its understanding of Jesus and of the Trinity. But the evidence does not point to the controversy being acute among Jewish Christians in the very earliest days of the church, let alone to Paul being a key figure in that controversy. The evidence of John, and probably of Paul's letter to the Colossians, suggests that this became an issue later rather than earlier, and in the Greek world rather than among Jewish Christians.

There is some evidence for John's Gospel being written in

the Ephesus area, in west Turkey, not far from Colosse. It is likely that, as the Christian message became separated in time and space from the Palestinian and Jewish context of the human Jesus and came into contact with Greco-Roman religions, all sorts of speculation about Jesus flourished. People did begin to interpret Jesus in terms of Greco-Roman spirituality, and acute questions about the divinity of Jesus were raised.

Second-century reports on the writing of the gospels

Papias, bishop of Hierapolis in Turkey, early second century:

"*Mark becoming Peter's interpreter wrote accurately all he remembered, though not in order, of the things said or done by the Lord... Matthew then put together the oracles in the Hebrew dialect.*"

Irenaeus, bishop of Lyons in France, late second century:

"*Luke, the follower of Paul, put down in a book the gospel preached by him. Then John, the disciple of the Lord... also published the gospel, while he was staying in Ephesus in Asia.*"

(All quoted from Eusebius, early Christian historian, book 3)

Rival gospels?

The Gnostic gospels

It is in this context that the so-called "gnostic gospels" need to be mentioned, because during the second and third centuries a number of gospels that are not in the Christian New Testament came to be written.

These gospels have recently attracted attention, for example when the media showed great interest in the "Gospel of Judas". The idea has become popular that these gospels were rivals to the ones we have in the New Testament, and that they were suppressed by the church in favour of the supposedly Pauline gospels.

This view has been popularized by writers such as Dan Brown. His bestseller *The Da Vinci Code* portrayed the fictional Sir Leigh Teabing quoting from "The Gospel of Philip" and claiming that Jesus married Mary Magdalene and had a child with her.[13] Teabing claims that this "fact" was suppressed by the church, as were the gospels that propounded such views.

The fictional Teabing's views are almost as fictional as he is himself. The Gospel of Philip does exist and, although the text is damaged at that point, it probably does refer to Jesus kissing Mary Magdalene, though not to any marriage or child. But the gospel has no historical credibility, and probably dates from well into the second century AD.

This gospel and others like it reflect the sort of speculative thinking that developed in the second-century "gnostic" movement, which offered spiritual freedom through "knowledge" (*gnosis* in Greek) of divine secrets and mysteries. Gnosticism reflects Greek and pagan thought, which tended to see the physical and material worlds as evil and transitory, and the spiritual world as true reality. Such thinking also arose within Christianity and gave rise to a variety of ideas – people denied the physical humanity of Jesus, seeing him as a solely divine being, and advocated an ascetic spirituality. Gospels such as the Gospel of Philip have nothing like those of the New Testament, which are clearly rooted in the historical situation of first-century Palestine. The Gnostic gospels have moved out of history into a world of philosophical and mystical fantasy. Jesus is more a mystical superman than a real historical person.

The Gnostic gospels were never serious rivals to the gospels of the New Testament. The idea that the Council of Nicaea in AD 325, which established the contents of the New Testament, had a whole range of gospels to choose from and accepted into the New Testament the ones that suited its theology is quite without foundation. The gospels of the New Testament go back to the first century, and had a recognized authority from the early second century, if not before; whereas the Gnostic gospels had no comparable claim. There was no conspiracy in favour of orthodoxy, however disappointing this may be for some people.

The Gnostic gospels are irrelevant to our question about Paul. The beginnings of Gnostic thinking can be recognized in the New Testament period; Paul and John argue against it, for example when Paul firmly rejects some of the ascetic tendencies of the Corinthian Christians. But the Gnostic gospels do not in any way bear witness to a strand of early Christianity that did not affirm the divinity of Christ; their tendency was, on the contrary, to deny his humanity and turn him into a purely spiritual being.

Jewish Christian gospels

Much more relevant to our question is the small number of Jewish Christian gospels that we know of: the Gospel of the Nazarenes, the Gospel of the Hebrews, and the Gospel of the Ebionites. We do not have these gospels, only odd snippets and quotations from them, but we know that they existed. The Ebionites were a group in the second century who denied the divinity of Jesus, and their gospel will have reflected their views. But there is no evidence that they represented an original Christian doctrine that was then corrupted by Paul.

There is no reason to think that the gospels of the Nazarenes and the Hebrews were Ebionite in outlook. The difficulty with them is that we have hardly any evidence of what they contained, just a few sayings and phrases quoted by others; and we do not know when and by whom they were written. The uncertainty about these gospels does not outweigh all the other and much clearer evidence that we have gathered about the beginnings of the Christian church and about the views of Jesus held by the strongly Jewish Christian Matthew.

There is also the evidence of the New Testament letter of James, probably written by James the brother of Jesus, which, rather like Matthew's Gospel, seems to be correcting misunderstandings of Paul's teaching about faith and good works, but which begins with James describing himself as a "servant of God and of the Lord Jesus Christ", in a way that reminds us very much of Paul.[14]

Conclusion

The idea that the New Testament is the product of a theological takeover by Paul makes for good fiction, but is without any solid basis at all. Even Mark and Luke, who were very likely companions of Paul, were not programmed by Paul, but had their own good sources of information. And the idea that there were many gospels competing in the early days of the church, with only the Pauline gospels surviving and the others being killed off is pure, if entertaining, fantasy.

CHAPTER 10

But Paul Was Certainly a Controversialist

One more question needs brief consideration. It has been argued here that Paul was not an innovator but a faithful follower of Jesus. But are we not in danger of ignoring the evidence in the New Testament itself which does show that he was a controversialist, pioneering new ideas and willing to take provocative positions. The New Testament shows that Paul could be combative, not meek. Was he not a powerful figure who worked very hard to get his own way?

The answer to these questions must be yes. Paul was a very influential figure in early Christianity, and he did fight for views he believed in; it cannot always have been comfortable to work with him.

However, Paul did not invent either the idea of Jesus' divinity, or that of Jesus' saving death. The controversy in which he took a major part was nothing to do with these issues, but concerned the question of Gentiles becoming Christians.

In order to clarify this it will be helpful to look in more detail at some of the ideas already discussed in chapter 3.

Paul's early ministry and lack of influence

Paul was probably converted just two or three years after the death and resurrection of Jesus, in the very earliest days of the church. But he was an outsider who appears to have had very little influence on the development of the Christian movement in the years immediately following his conversion.

After his conversion Paul was hardly ever in Jerusalem, where the church was based: this was not surprising, given that the Jews saw him as someone who had betrayed them by going over to the Christians and then starting to evangelize Jews around the Mediterranean world. But even among some Christians in Jerusalem he was suspect. This was, first, because of his history as their arch-persecutor, and then later because of his missionary work among Gentiles and his questionable loyalty to the Jewish law (as some of the Jewish Christians saw it). So Paul's visits to Jerusalem were brief – he speaks of visits three years and fourteen years after his conversion,[1] and his influence on the leadership and direction of the Christian church was modest.

The leadership of the church in Jerusalem in those earliest days seems to have been in the hands of Peter and then of James, the brother of Jesus. Paul met both of them, as he tells us; but the visits were short, and there can be no doubt that they were the ones in charge and Paul was the outsider. He does speak of spending fifteen days with Peter three years after his conversion, but it is probable that he was the learner and not the teacher. It is very unlikely that Paul, then or afterwards, started propagating a novel view of Jesus that was radically different from the views of Peter and James.

One of the recurrent themes in Paul's letters is the question of his status in the church: he was not one of the twelve apostles, who were trained and authorized by Jesus in his ministry, and yet he believed that he did have something like the same status, having been called by Jesus on the Damascus road. In his letter to the Galatians he describes how he was duly recognized as leader of the mission to the Gentiles by the Jerusalem church leaders.[2] But it is clear that this claim was not accepted by everyone. He was and remained something of an outsider, whose views were treated with suspicion by some. What Paul said was not necessarily accepted, and his views would certainly not have taken hold if they were obviously unorthodox.

In due course Paul did become a key and influential leader of Gentile churches, based in Antioch in Syria. But that still did not make him someone who could – or did – change the mind of the whole Christian church on their fundamental understanding of Jesus. He was not a proto-Pope, even among Gentile churches.

Paul was also not the person who brought the Christian gospel to Rome, and when he writes to the Christians in Rome he sounds slightly tentative, because he knows that he does not have authority there. Paul also did not have anything to do with the spread of Christianity in the East, in Mesopotamia and beyond.

The founding of the Roman church

We do not know who founded the church in Rome or exactly when. It could possibly have been Peter. But there is interesting evidence of Christians being in Rome in AD 49. The Roman historian Suetonius, not a Christian, tells us that the Emperor Claudius expelled the Jewish community from Rome then, because they were "rioting at the instigation of Chrestus".This communal expulsion is also referred to in the New Testament book of Acts.We do not know for certain who "Chrestus" was or what the rioting was about. But the best guess is that there were disturbances in the Jewish community over "Christ"; they were so acute that the emperor had an excuse for some ethnic cleansing of Jews (and Jewish Christians like Aquila and Priscilla) from Rome. It is quite clear from Luke's honest account in Acts that Christianity was a divisive and disturbing influence among the Jews, which makes sense if the Christians were claiming that Jesus was not only the messiah, but also divine.

The Gentile mission

Where Paul was influential was over the question of the Gentiles.

The Christian movement was a missionary one from the start, with Jesus sending out the apostles to tell people the good news of God's kingdom. The word "apostle" itself means "one who is sent", and is not far in meaning from our word "missionary". Jesus sent out the twelve apostles to announce to the world that God's reign (God's kingdom) was breaking into history in a new way. Jesus worked largely among the Jews of Palestine, and so did his apostles.

But after Jesus' death his followers started meeting Gentiles and sharing the good news of Jesus with them.

The question then was: if Gentiles want to be followers of Jesus and members of God's kingdom, what should they do? Was it enough for them to be baptized, like Jews who became Christians? Or did they need also to become Jews, being circumcised and keeping all the Jewish law? This was an acute dilemma. For some of the Christians in Jerusalem, who had been Jews all their lives and who lived in the staunchly Jewish city, it was clear that all converts should become Christian Jews or Jewish Christians. But for those who were working with Gentiles, for example in the big Syrian city of Antioch (modern Antakya) it was not so obvious at all.

This was a theological issue of great importance, but also a painfully practical issue – painful for Gentile converts who might need to be circumcised! But it was painful also for Jewish Christians in Jerusalem, who could be seen by their fellow Jews as traitors if they accepted Gentiles without conversion to Judaism. It was also an issue of great historical importance: would Christianity be one sect within Judaism (like the Pharisees or the sect that produced the Dead Sea Scrolls), or would it be something bigger?

It is this issue that appears to have been the most divisive in the early days of the church, and much of the New Testament can be seen to have been written with it in mind. Paul himself was very involved in the debate, and became the most prominent leader of the mission to the Gentiles and the most forceful theological exponent of what might be called the "liberal" viewpoint. His letters engage with this controversy again and again, with Paul becoming heated in his advocacy of Christian freedom. He insisted that Jesus, through his death, had brought to an end the era of sacrifice, of the Temple, and of Jewish ritual; he believed that Jesus had inaugurated a new era of relating to God through Jesus himself and the Holy Spirit.[3]

Paul by no means saw the coming of Jesus as meaning the abolition of Judaism or a new start. On the contrary, Jesus was the messiah, who represented the fulfilment of Israel's hopes and of the Old Testament story. But on the question of the law, which had been so all-important for him as a Pharisee, Paul did believe that the era of the law had been superseded by the era of the Spirit.

Paul did not carry the day on these matters without struggle. He came into conflict not just with the very conservative Jewish Christians in Jerusalem, but also, at one point, with Peter, the first leader of the church. He also fell out over the matter with his colleague Barnabas, who had generously sponsored and encouraged him in the early days of his ministry. However, the outcome of the struggles was acceptance of Paul's views by Peter and the main leaders of the church, though it was agreed that there should be sensitivity towards Jewish Christians who had scruples and difficulties about freedom from the law.[4]

Paul's desire to agree with the leaders of the Jerusalem church

What is clear from Paul's own letters is that he was convinced of the rightness of his views on this matter, but also that it mattered to him that the senior leaders of the church, such as Peter and James, the brother of Jesus, did recognize and support his views. He actually speaks at one point of putting his "gospel" to the leaders of the Jerusalem church, "lest I had run in vain" – in case he had got everything wrong. He cared about what the apostles of Jesus believed, and his gospel was about Jesus bringing unity between God and humanity and between people. "There is neither Jew nor Greek... you are all one in Christ Jesus" was not just a theory for him, but was a practical priority to which he was committed.[5]

One of Paul's major projects, to which he refers in his letters, was a charitable collection for the Christians in Jerusalem, since Paul was keen for Jews and Gentiles to stand together and to love each other.[6] It is important to see that Paul was not a cheerful innovator who did not care if he went off in a different theological direction from others.

The question of the Gentile mission was a controversial one, partly because it had not arisen very much or very directly in Jesus' ministry. Jesus focused his work on "the lost sheep of the house of Israel" – his fellow Jews. He challenged the inward-looking prejudices of his contemporaries (for example against Samaritans) at the same time and had a vision for God's kingdom extending to everyone, not just the Jews of Palestine. But Jesus said very little with any bearing on what might be expected of Gentiles becoming Christians.

As for the law, Jesus seems to have been very positive about the Old Testament and interpreted his own mission in that context, though he was much more relaxed about issues such as the Sabbath and ritual washing than his Pharisaic opponents, to their annoyance. But the question of whether Gentiles should be required to keep the law was one that he never addressed directly. The nearest he came to this was in his references to the Jewish laws concerning clean and unclean food, which Mark saw as Jesus "cleansing" those foods; Paul probably had the same saying in mind when he wrote that "in the Lord Jesus... nothing is unclean".[7]

So when, after Jesus' death and resurrection, the Christian church started to reach out to Gentiles, there were no indisputable teachings as to what to do about them and what should be required of them. It was in a sense a "new" question with which the early Christian leaders had to wrestle. Paul's contribution to the discussion was vital.

Paul as a person

Paul could and did play an active part in the controversy over the Gentiles, even falling out temporarily with colleagues and friends. But the view that Paul was a characteristically arrogant person and difficult to live with is not supported by the evidence. When he fought, it was with words and ideas, rather than using physical force as in his pre-conversion days. He sometimes became emotional and forceful in his letters because he cared deeply about the Christ whom he had met on the Damascus road: so he saw the imposition of the old Jewish law on Gentile converts as undermining the point of Jesus' crucifixion. And because he cared greatly for people he wanted them to know and experience the grace of God, as he had in his conversion experience, and not to be forced back into the old religion of law-keeping, from which he had been saved.

In his letters Paul comes over as someone with real affection for those to whom he wrote, and someone whom others loved and cared for. He was conscious of being called to lead, but he also worked well with others, encouraging and helping them. In the final chapter of his letter to the Romans he greets all sorts of old friends, such as Priscilla and Aquila, speaking warmly and appreciatively of them.

Paul was uncontroversial in his view of Jesus

Paul did contend strongly over the matter of the Gentiles, and contributed vitally to the discussion about it. But it is not obvious that he argued in the same way over the question of Jesus' identity and divinity, or even over the question of the death of Jesus. Nor is it obvious that he, as an outsider and a latecomer apostle (who had converted when the church was already in being) would have had a legitimate claim to make such a contribution, whereas on the "new" question of the Gentiles he had a clear and legitimate interest.

The evidence suggests that Jesus' divinity was not a doctrine superimposed on the story of Jesus artificially by Paul or by anyone else; it was a conclusion that emerged from how people experienced Jesus during his ministry and from the experience of Jesus himself. It was the story of Jesus that generated the idea of his divinity, not the idea that generated the story. The conclusion that he was divine arose out of his amazing life and teaching, out of his evident closeness to God as his "Abba", and above all out of his resurrection.

Paul was responsible for none of these factors. He accepted the early Christian view of Jesus through his conversion experience. Of course, his experience gave him a first-hand way into Christian ideas – it was a real divine revelation, as he believed. But what he discovered was not something novel or original to him. He discovered that the first Christians were right about Jesus the messiah, about Jesus as the one risen from the dead, and about Jesus as Lord.

So it is true that Paul was a controversialist. But whereas there is ample evidence for his involvement in the Gentile controversy, there is no evidence of comparable controversy over the divinity and death of Jesus. He received what other Christians before him passed on to him, and he passed that on to others.

CHAPTER 11

So Did Paul Get Jesus Right?

To view the historical Jesus as a fine but entirely human Jewish teacher, and to ascribe some of the strange and supernatural aspects of the Christian Jesus to the imagination of Paul or others in the early church is undoubtedly an appealing idea to some people. It provides ammunition for those who wish to discredit Christianity if they can show that there was such a fundamental ideological conflict at the very beginning; but it is also positively attractive to others as a way of rescuing what they see as a credible Jesus from his Pauline captivity.

A century ago the eccentric but brilliant thinker Albert Schweitzer argued that the theologians of his day, for all their claimed objectivity, were interpreting Jesus in ways that suited their own preferences and outlook rather than with historical objectivity. And George Tyrrell commented that people were looking down the well of history trying to see the real Jesus but what they were seeing was, of course, a reflection of their own faces. The danger is just the same today, that people – Christians and others – will read their own agenda into their interpretation of Jesus, whether consciously or unconsciously.

The argument of this book, written by a Christian seeking to be as objective as possible, is that there is very good evidence against the idea that Paul was the inventor or imaginer of the divine Jesus.

He was a very important figure in early Christianity, who probably did more than anyone else to make the Christian church an international movement – with strongly Jewish roots but with a universal outlook and practice. His letters, though they are not always easy to understand, represent remarkable insight into how the religion of Jesus of Nazareth, which started within the Jewish context of Galilee and Jerusalem, could speak to and be relevant to the non-Jewish world of the first-century Roman empire. But he did not invent either the idea of Jesus' divinity, or the idea of Jesus' saving death.

It is worth summing up the journey that leads to this conclusion.

Chapter 1 introduced the question and explained its importance.

Chapter 2 laid the foundation for the rest of the book by explaining why the New Testament may be seen as a credible historical source. It is corroborated by non-Christian sources, and all the books of the New Testament were written in the first century, close to the time of Jesus.

Chapter 3 looked at Paul's conversion experience on the Damascus road and argued that it did not produce an inventor, but a humble and grateful "slave of Jesus Christ".

Chapters 4 to 6 showed that, contrary to some people's impressions, Paul was very familiar with many of the stories and sayings of Jesus. He knew about the crucifixion, about the Last Supper that Jesus had with his disciples, about the resurrection of Jesus and his subsequent appearances, about his closeness to God as Father. He knew teaching and parables of Jesus, including his teaching on divorce, on apostleship, on his future "second coming", and on love. He passed on the stories of Jesus to others and regarded them as authoritative. He was creative, not wooden, in interpreting the teaching for new situations; but his starting-point was Jesus and Jesus' words.

Chapter 7 considered the origins of Paul's belief in the divinity of Jesus and in the atoning significance of his death, and found strong reasons for thinking that those central Christian doctrines pre-dated Paul's conversion, and indeed had their roots in Jesus' own life and teaching, and in the church's experience of Jesus rising from the dead.

Chapter 8 looked rather more widely at Jesus and Paul and at differences between them, concluding that their differences were real and understandable (in terms of their different contexts), but that they were in accord on the essentials.

Chapter 9 responded to the idea that the New Testament represents a Pauline spin on Jesus and early Christianity, and argued that there is every reason to see the gospels in the New Testament (but not other gospels) as genuine early accounts of the Christian beginnings that were not derived from Paul.

Chapter 10 agreed that Paul was a controversialist who was influential in the development of the Christian church. But his doctrinal contribution was to the discussion of Gentiles and Jews in the Christian church, not to questions of Jesus' divinity and crucifixion.

Paul's positive witness to Jesus

The fact that Paul did not imagine or invent the Christian doctrines of the divinity of Jesus and of his atoning death is a negative conclusion – about a wrong but rather common modern idea. But it is also a positive conclusion about the origins of Christianity, because if Paul is not the inventor of the divine Jesus, he is a remarkable witness to him. How so?

1. The early date of Paul's witness

The letters of Paul are widely and justifiably regarded as the earliest writings in the New Testament, and thus as the earliest written evidence for Christianity. And they are very early: Paul's letter to the Galatians is plausibly dated to around AD 48, his first letter to the Thessalonians to AD 50, and his first letter to the Corinthians to AD 55. Jesus was crucified under Pontius Pilate, probably in AD 30, give or take a year or two. So there is written Christian evidence for Jesus from within twenty years of his death; assertions about the New Testament being written hundreds of years after Jesus are ill-informed indeed.

2. The gospel of Jesus, the Son of God

The evidence of Paul's letters is quite clear about the main outlines of the Christian message that was being preached, rather successfully, by Paul and others in the Mediterranean world of the time. It was a message about Jesus of Nazareth as Son of God, about his death through crucifixion bringing forgiveness of sins, about his resurrection from the dead, and about his expected return to earth. There is no reasonable doubt that this was the Christian gospel at the time.

3. Paul's message is like the New Testament gospels

There is, as this book has shown, a lot of evidence to suggest that Paul's version of the gospel included much more than the key elements above, and that he knew details of the life, death, resurrection, and teaching of Jesus. There is, in fact, a good case for saying that the "good news" of Jesus as preached and taught by Paul was rather similar to the "good news" as we now find it in the gospels.[1] The gospel of Luke, coming as it probably does from a companion of Paul, surely gives us insight into what Paul and those working with him said and taught about Jesus.

The gospels may not have been written until the AD 60s or later, but Paul suggests that the kinds of story they tell were being passed on some years earlier than that.

4. Paul received the gospel in the AD 30s

The suggestion that the good news preached by Paul was quite like the written gospels of the New Testament could, after all, seem to lend weight to the argument that Paul was the originator of the gospel story as we know it. But there is no evidence whatsoever that the main ingredients of

Paul's gospel – in particular his teaching about Jesus' life, death, and resurrection – were unique to him or disputed by others. Indeed the evidence points to Paul having "received" the gospel from others, and then "passed it on" when he went to places such as Galatia, Thessalonica, and Corinth. This is very significant: Paul founded these churches several years before writing his letters to them, and so we have evidence that this was the gospel he passed on at that time.

Even more significantly, Paul speaks of "receiving the gospel" himself, and this goes right back to the time of his conversion in the AD 30s. This cannot be proved, but it does suggest that the Christian good news about Jesus' atoning death and resurrection as God's divine Son goes right back to the beginning of the Christian era, and that it did not originate with Paul. Indeed Paul's ferocious hostility to the Christians before his conversion surely arose because the claims being made for Jesus were highly offensive to him as a zealous Jew, not just because Jesus was a prophet with mildly liberal views.

5. The earliest written gospel is in Paul's letters
Even if it cannot be proved exactly what Paul "received", or when, or how, it is certain that the earliest Christian gospel to which we have access is that reflected and attested in Paul's letters. People are excited by the discovery of new gospels – such as the Gospel of Thomas or the Gospel of Judas – and when they hear scholars speculating about the possible importance of these discoveries. But although the popular media seize on such stories and make much of them, there is frequently little or no substance in their claims. It is just possible that the Gospel of Thomas

contains one or two genuine sayings of Jesus that are not
preserved in the canonical gospels, but it is uncertain,
and other non-canonical gospels have even less claim to
credibility. By contrast, the evidence of Paul is very reliable
on the Christian gospel he preached and received. His
version of the gospel does not just go back to the first
century, but to shortly after the life of Christ. It is the
earliest Christian gospel that we have.

6. Paul is an intelligent, knowledgeable witness

The purpose of this book is not to prove that Jesus was
divine, but to disprove the assertion that Paul imagined
this idea or other ideas about Jesus. However, there is
no question that Paul is a most significant witness to the
truth of the New Testament gospels and to the divine
Jesus whom they describe. Paul was a highly intelligent and
educated man, who was studying in Jerusalem when the
Christian movement began in the early AD 30s. He started
out thoroughly sceptical about Jesus of Nazareth and about
the claims that the Christians were making for him. Paul
will have heard the Christian arguments and debated with
those proposing them; he will have known and exploited
every weakness in the Christians' case. But then his mind
was changed through his Damascus road experience. He
became a completely convinced advocate of the Christian
view of Jesus. He still knew all the arguments against
the Christian case, but he now saw that that his previous
assessment of them was completely wrong. After his
conversion he met people who had known Jesus very well
during his lifetime, such as Peter and James, but also many
others.

Of course, it is possible to argue that Paul became deranged through whatever he experienced on the Damascus road, and that he then lived his life on the basis of a psychologically induced fantasy. We know that people do sometimes have fantastic religious delusions. However, Paul is not so easily dismissed: after his conversion he does not come across as deranged in any way, but as someone who continued to be a highly intelligent and balanced person of great integrity. And when he speaks of Jesus, for example of his resurrection, he does not just appeal to his own overwhelmingly convincing experience, but refers to many other people who saw Jesus, including Peter, James, and others. Paul was not a mad individualist who invented the divine Jesus, but someone who came to accept the amazing fact that others before him had recognized: namely Jesus of Nazareth was divine and did die for his sins and for the sins of the world.

People have sometimes said that there are only three ways of making sense of Jesus and his ministry – either he was bad, or he was mad, or he was God. Something similar might be said about Paul, and perhaps more persuasively. It could be that he deliberately created his own religion using, or rather abusing, the religion of Jesus to further his own ends. Or he might not have been deliberately manipulative but mentally deluded, living the rest of his life after the conversion experience in the light of his delusion and sharing it with others. However, neither of these views is convincing: the evidence points toward the third view, that Paul was a soberly intelligent person, of real integrity, whose conversion turned him into a serious follower of Jesus as the Son of God. He gave his life to passing on the good news to others because he believed that it mattered eternally and that it was true.

Notes

Chapter 1
1. London: Green, 1907.
2. London: Weidenfeld, 1986.
3. My earlier books *Paul and Jesus: The True Story*, London: SPCK, 2002, and especially *Paul: Follower of Jesus or Founder of Christianity?*, Grand Rapids: Eerdmans, 1999, go into much greater detail, looking at different views and other evidence.

Chapter 2
1. Acts 18:2.
2. Luke 1:3.

Chapter 3
1. Acts 1:1.
2. Colossians 4:14.
3. The "we" passages start at Acts 16.
4. Galatians 1:13, 14
5. Galatians 1:13
6. Acts 8:3.
7. Acts 9:1–19.
8. Acts 9:13,14, 26.
9. 2 Corinthians 11:25, Acts 28.
10. Acts 9:20.
11. Galatians 1:16.
12. Galatians 1:11.
13. Galatians 1:23.
14. 1 Timothy 1:15.
15. Romans 1:1, Philippians 3:6–10.

Chapter 4
1. 1 Corinthians 11:23–25.
2. 1 Corinthians 5:7.
3. Galatians 3:1.
4. Galatians 6:17.
5. 1 Corinthians 15:8–9.
6. For the New Testament evidence see Acts 18.
7. See 1 Corinthians 11.

Chapter 5

1. 1 Corinthians 7:7, 17.
2. 1 Corinthians 7:5.
3. 1 Corinthians 7:10, 11.
4. 1 Corinthians 7:12.
5. Mark 10:9–12.
6. 1 Corinthians 7:15.
7. 1 Corinthians 9:14.
8. Luke 10:7, Matthew 10:10.
9. 1 Corinthians 9:12.
10. 1 Corinthians 9:18,19.
11. Mark 10:43–45.
12. John 13.
13. Galatians 5:13, 6:2.
14. Matthew 5:44, Luke 6:27, 28, Matthew 10:25–37, Romans 12:14.
15. 1 Corinthians 13.
16. John 13:34–35.
17. John 13:1–17.
18. See Michael Gorman, *Cruciformity*, Grand Rapids: Eerdmans, 2001.

Chapter 6

1. Galatians 4:4–6.
2. Romans 8:15.
3. Mark 14:36.
4. 1 Thessalonians 1:9–11.
5. 1 Corinthians 16:22.
6. 1 Thessalonians 1:10.
7. 1 Thessalonians 4:13.
8. 1 Thessalonians 4:14, 15.
9. 1 Thessalonians 5:1, 2.
10. Matthew 24:42–44.
11. Matthew 25:1–13.

Chapter 7

1. *The God Delusion*, London: Bantam, 2006, 252.
2. 1 Corinthians 1:13–23.
3. Mark 2:15–17, Luke 15:1, 2.
4. 1 Corinthians 15:1–3.
5. Exodus 24:6.
6. 1 Corinthians 1:3.
7. 1 Corinthians 8:6.
8. Colossians 1:15–20.
9. 1 Corinthians 15:14.
10. Romans 1:3,4.
11. Philippians 2:6–11.
12. Acts 2:36.

13. On the resurrection a major scholarly discussion of the evidence is N. T. Wright, *The Resurrection of the Son of God*, London: SPCK, 2003.

14. Deuteronomy 6:4.

15. Psalms 2:7, 2 Samuel 7:14.

16. John 1:1.

17. Colossians 1:15–20, 1 Corinthians 1:24.

18. His *One God, One Lord*, London: SCM, 1998, is one of the most important discussions of the origin of the idea of Jesus' divinity.

Chapter 8

1. For example Mark 1:15.

2. Isaiah 52:7.

3. Mark 3:22–29.

4. Matthew 6:10, 13:1–33, 24:45–25:30.

5. Romans 1:3–4.

6. Romans 1:17–18, 3:21.

7. 1 Corinthians 6:9.

8. 1 Corinthians 4:20.

9. Romans 14:17.

10. Acts 17:7.

11. Romans 1:17.

12. Mark 2:17, Luke 15:4–7.

13. Luke 4:18, 16:19–31.

14. Luke 10:25–42.

15. Romans 15:7.

16. 1 Corinthians 1:26.

17. Romans 16:23.

18. Galatians 3:28.

19. Ephesians 6:5–9, Colossians 3:22–4:1.

20. Romans 16:1–7; 1 Corinthians 11.

21. *God is Not Great*, London: Atlantic, 2007, 54.

22. 1 Corinthians 11:1–16, 14:34–35, 1 Timothy 2:11–15.

23. So he uses the Old Testament book of Genesis in 1 Corinthians 6:16, 11:8, 9, and elsewhere.

24. He discusses the body at length in 1 Corinthians 6:12–20.

25. 1 Corinthians 11:1.

26. Luke 10:29–37, Matthew 5–7.

27. Matthew 5:27–32, 19:1–12.

28. Mark 10:17–31, Luke 12:33.

29. Matthew 5:43–48.

30. Luke 11:4.

31. Matthew 19:26.

32. Matthew 7:13–14.

33. For example Matthew 23, Luke 16:19–31.

34. 1 Corinthians 6:12, 10:23.

35. Philippians 1:10, 11.

36. 1 Corinthians 13:1–3.

37. Daniel 7.
38. Mark 11:1–10, Zechariah 9:9.
39. Mark 15:9–12, 26.
40. Matthew 15:24, Romans 1:16.
41. 1 Corinthians 16:22, Matthew 24:45–51, 22:41–45.
42. Romans 5, 1 Corinthians 15.
43. Galatians 2:20.

Chapter 9
1. So Acts 15:36–41. Those verses describe a falling-out of Paul and Mark, but Colossians 4:10 suggests that that parting of the ways was only temporary.
2. Matthew 1:23.
3. Matthew 28:16–20.
4. Mark 2:1–12, 6:45–52, 13:32.
5. Matthew 5:17.
6. Matthew 5:19.
7. Grand Rapids: Eerdmans 2006.
8. Mark 15:21.
9. Luke 1:1–4.
10. 1 John 1:18,19.
11. John 1:1–14.
12. John 21:20–24.
13. *The Da Vinci Code* (London: Bantam, 2004).
14. James 1:1.

Chapter 10
1. Galatians 1.
2. Galatians 2, see also 1 Corinthians 15:9.
3. His letters to the Galatians and the Romans are those that engage most with the issue.
4. The struggles are described most fully in Galatians 2 and Acts 15.
5. Galatians 2:2, 3:28.
6. 2 Corinthians 8–9.
7. Mark 7:18,19, Romans 14:14.

Chapter 11
1. Paul's brief summary of "the gospel" in his letter to the Romans 1:1–4 is intriguingly like our gospels in its overall shape.